HANCEL
THEY DON'T BUY ME NO PEANUTS

I think you will enjoy this JD

A MEMIOR

BY

JULIA V. DAWSON

Julia V. Dawson
4/26/03

e-mail
juliadawson@tds.net

ISBN: 0-7596-5897-8   .

This book is printed on acid free paper.

First Edition

1stBooks - rev. 02/27/02

CHAPTERS

PROLOGUE

A millennium has ended, and a century has closed. A century spanning an era that went from the horse and buggy to the Space Age. Remembering the wondrous things that transpired during that time, the marvelous inventions and technology created, and discoveries made I thought of the material it would furnish for a book. My grandmother's and my mother's lives would provide fabric and plot. I reflected on the romances, the joys, jubilations and moments of despairs that filled their lives. I recalled tales I had heard, or half heard, in my childhood. As I began to write, and the words flowed, I realized that I, too, have lived from the horse and buggy to the Space Age.

My grandmother, Sadie, and incidents in her life are recorded as she related them, and from my memories and observations of her during her later years. She took pride in the fact that her ancestors crossed the mountains in a covered wagon. The early years of my mother, Hancel, are noted as she often recited them. My memories are intertwined but it is Hancel's story. It depicts the struggles and dire circumstances that surrounded her everyday life as a young widow, with five little children to support during the depression years.

The following subtitle is used to denote defiance and independence: "THEY DON'T BUY ME NO PEANUTS" was Hancel's favorite expression.

SADIE

Sadie was my grandmother. Not much is known about Sadie's early years. I know that she was born in Monticello, Indiana in 1876. She once mentioned that her mother had spoken of an early census that registered neighbors and friends as born in Ohio, New York, Pennsylvania, North Carolina, Germany, and Scotland. Their occupations were listed as shoemakers, wagon-makers, coopers, blacksmiths, railroad workers, schoolteachers and cabinetmakers.

She also recalled that life consisted of hard work and toil. She spoke of her school days with fondness, saying, "Those were hard times. I had to walk a long way to school. Many days, all I carried in my lunch bucket was a piece of dried pumpkin. We didn't have fancy lunch buckets, as children do today. We used old syrup buckets. In later years, we rode to school in a horse drawn school wagon. Seats were arranged on each side of the enclosed vehicle, below rows of windows. We often spied a fox or bobcat as we watched out the window. On cold days a wood stove, located near the rear of the wagon, provided heat. When fuel was exhausted, the driver stopped to pick up wood. He often called upon older boys to help him. My school days ended at the end of the sixth grade; which wasn't unusual in those days."

Once, as Sadie visited, while we were shopping at a large delicatessen shop, she spied dried fish in the showcase. She asked me to buy some, as she reminisced, "During the winter, we usually had dried fish for Sunday dinners. Dad called it "Finnie Haddie." He bought it by the barrel full and carted it home from Fort Wayne. It was usually my chore to reach in the bottom of the barrel and take out six pieces and put them to soak before they were cooked."

Sadie grew to be a beautiful young lady. Her stepfather, Edward Kirk, owned a livery stable and wagon making shop. A city gentleman, a regular customer at the establishment, had

1

frequently noticed Sadie. His wife needed a live in maid and cook helper. He asked if Sadie could come to work for them, saying that she would be treated like one of the family. Sadie liked the idea of earning money of her own, and it would allow her to occupy her time. In those days work as a domestic was about the only employment available for young women. She accepted the offer. On one of her frequent trips home she mentioned that she was not allowed to eat at the table with the family, and was only admitted through the back door. As she enumerated the many chores she was required to perform, her mother doubted that she was being treated like one of the family; in fact she thought she was being over worked. She made her come home.

Sadie soon sparked the interest of William Chappel, who was an employee in her father's shop as a wagon maker. He began inviting Sadie out for walks and found various reasons to be in her company. He soon became a regular visitor in their home. Her parents noticed that he seemed to take more than a casual interest in their daughter. When they conveyed their thoughts to Sadie, she thought them wrong saying, "He is much older than I am." However, she found herself looking forward to his visits.

One Sunday, as they were out for a stroll, William said, "I've been looking for a place to open a cabinet shop. I have found what I believe to be the ideal spot in Remington. I have given your father notice that I will be leaving his employment. I have also told him that I am in love with you and intend to ask you to marry me. Will you marry me, Sadie?

Sadie demurred. "I don't know if I love you. I'm not even sure that I know what love is. I do know that I enjoy being in your company. I like being with you."

"You can learn to love me. More than one successful marriage has been based on friendship. But I sense more than friendship in our relationship. Marry me, Sadie." Before long,

Sadie realized their friendship had developed into love. They were wed.

America was prospering. It was a country on the move. Railroads beckoned and lured. William traveled to Illinois to meet with an attorney and complete details for obtaining a patent on his invention for a mail bag, that would hang suspended from a crane mounted on a metal post, to be used for quick mail pick up at stations that had no regular stops. Returning home he related tales of his trip. "I stayed in a fashionable hotel that had a Regina Music Box in the lobby. Being a cabinetmaker, it interested me greatly. It was an ornate wooden cabinet with a metal disk inside. The disk was perforated with small dots and a series of slots. When a wheel rotated, tiny tines, or forks, circulated over the disk creating music. The detailed workmanship, as well as the instrument itself, fascinated me." William's patent was issued in January of 1894.

Sadie settled into married life. Her hours were filled with harmony and contentment. She told her mother, "William is considerate and gentle. He pleases me in many ways but bells do not ring, nor does my heart palpitate."

"There is much to be said for contentment. Love does not always mean bells ringing. Such emotion will only fade with time. Just be glad that your man is good and steady."

William was tall and thin. His hair was prematurely streaked with gray. His long, tapered fingers were digits suitable for a surgeon or pianist. It was a daily ritual keeping pumice powder and linseed oil cleaned from under his nails, and brown stain off his hands. He often used walnut husks to hand rub stain on furniture.

Sadie, although tall, was a head shorter than William. Her chestnut brown hair curled slightly and was usually wore in a chignon at the nape of her neck, or loosely tied with a ribbon. William liked it best when it was hanging loose. She sewed her own dresses and usually wore soft pastel colors. Her luminous brown eyes reflected sadness. She was shy and reticent around people, but warm and friendly as one became acquainted with her. She was neither meek nor submissive but usually deferred to Williams's judgment in matters of importance. However, if an opinion was set in her mind, it was sometime difficult to dissuade her. Due to her Scottish ancestry, she was inclined to be thrifty. She pondered deeply before spending money. In matters of money, William was disposed to be impulsive and to spend freely.

They lived in upstairs rooms, above the furniture store. Business, although not booming, provided a good living. Sadie was looking forward to the birth of her first child. On the twenty-seventh day of January, 1895 a baby girl arrived. She was named Hancel Fern Chappel. Hancel was my mother.

Hancel

HANCEL

Hancel was born into an era of change. A new century was about to begin, a Century of Progress. During her life span many new and unique inventions would be forth coming. Although the Indians had followed their trail of tears across the Mississippi River, a few braves were still causing trouble in the west. "Remember the Maine" became the war cry after the battleship Maine was blown up in Manila Bay. The Rough Riders charged up San Juan Hill when Cuba's rebellion against Spanish rule entangled, and involved, the United States. Thomas Edison invented a projector that produced moving pictures, and electric lights appeared on the scene. She would even witness that giant leap for mankind on the surface of the moon, as it was televised.

Sadie's Young Ladies Journal reported: "The population of London exceeds every city in the world, both ancient or modern. Scotland, Switzerland, and the Australian colonies combined have fewer souls." Another tid-bit, and reported as cold fact, stated: "The busy bee works for only three hours per day. It's reputation for sobriety is little deserved, especially if there is a cider mill close by. They fly off, buzz around the mill sipping up cider until full. They stay out all night and become disorderly and boisterous."

Lydia Pinkham's vegetable compound was toted as a cure all for female weaknesses and melancholia. A yard of dress gingham could be purchased for five cents per yard. Activities centered on the family, Sunday picnics in the park, Fourth of July parades, band concerts, rides on a bicycle built for two, visiting aunts and uncles and trips to grandma's house.

The baby slept in a bassinet. William, realizing that she was outgrowing it, toiled laboriously and secretly long into the night making a new crib for her. Sadie quickly realized that if she needed an item of furniture she had only to mention it to William and he would make it. (Their first kitchen table, refinished and refurbished, is still in use today in a great, great grandson's home.)

Natural gas was discovered in Upland, Indiana in 1888, with new wells coming in weekly. By 1891 the town was booming. By the 1900s gas fields covered thousands of square miles. Factories were given free gas, and often free land, for building in many areas. New cities and towns sprang up and existing ones expanded; towns like Muncie, Anderson, Gas City, Mt. Zion and Matthews. Matthews boomed and built more saloons than churches. The founding fathers dreamed of becoming the new capital of Indiana and built wide streets to accommodate the anticipated flow of traffic. Manufacturing plants, especially glass houses, drew glass blowers, artisans, businessmen, and bankers. They also attracted criminals and prostitutes. Ornate pleasure houses operated and flourished at the edge of these cities.

One day William came home and announced, "I think that we should move to Upland, in Grant County, Indiana. The population of the town, as well as the county, is growing rapidly. A few years ago I built a hearse for the little community, which is now bustling with activity. Factories are booming in the area. There will be a demand for carpenters and cabinetmakers. Would you object to relocating?"

"I see that you are excited by the prospects of moving. The decision is yours to make. I will abide by it.

"I think it would be a wise move. If agreeable, I will begin making arrangements to move."

In due time the move was made. Sadie found it interesting to discover that the small settlement had been carved out of dense forest. Old timers told that when they arrived the forest was so thick one could hardly see the sky for the trees. Some recalled a cluster of cabins, once located in an area, known as Rising Sun, which lay at the edge of the forest. It was so named be use it was the first place the sun could be seen upon exiting dense

7

woods. In 1829 settlers began to arrive; soldiers who had fought in the Revolution and received Bounty Lands, deeded by Andrew Jackson, for their war service. The first road rambled around bogs, tree stumps and chuck holes. On rainy days they were filled with mud. The first major road was an old trail that led from Richmond to Fort Wayne called the "Quaker Trace." With the coming of the railroad in 1867, and the promise of daily train stops, the town was platted. The first railroad was built from Union City to Logansport. (It was later know as the Pennsylvania Railroad)

Hancel often recalled the hearse that William had made. "It was an ornate, black box like conveyance, with glass windows on the side which were draped with gray satin. The inside walls and ceiling were tufted and padded with the same material. The outside was ornately scrolled. Two horses pulled the hearse while the driver sat perched high up on a seat at the front of the vehicle, behind the horse's staves.

It's hard to tell exactly the year in which William and Sadie arrived in Upland. An old census report shows them living in Remington (Jasper County) Indiana in 1900. It listed two daughters, Hancel and Vivian and a son, Albert. Albert was William's son by a previous marriage. That same census also listed Dora Paulina Kirk (Sadie's mother) living as the head of another household; an indication that her husband had died.

The 1910 census of Upland, Jefferson Township, Grant county, Indiana lists the family to include two sons, Jay and Burdett. Albert was not listed. An old photo of a church, built in the early 1900s in Upland, noted pictured members including Dora Kirk and Vivian Chappel. This also indicated that Sadie's mother might have moved with them.

The town was the highest point on the Pennsylvania Railroad between Chicago and Columbus, Ohio. A twenty-five foot ravine was dug through the center of the town to accommodate for the grade of the tracks. It divided the town. Sadie remembered that the townspeople earned an assessment, leveled against their property, by laying sod along the high banks. In time, three wooden bridges were erected over the tracks. The main bridge sat by the station house. Shelters were built over two stairways leading down to double tracks below. Passengers had to descend the stairs to board the trains. Eight trains ran daily during the peak of rail travel.

Hancel found it difficult to adjust to the town whistles. The government signal office relayed weather conditions over telegraph wires. They then signaled the townspeople. A toot of the whistle indicated threatening weather. It might warn of a tornado approaching; rain in the summer or snow in the winter. The whistle blew for curfew, and town functions evolved around the toot of the whistle.

It was a time of wild fancies, of flying machines and automobiles. The Wright brothers were perfecting their first successful airplane, the "Bird of Prey." They foolishly suggested that some-day planes would carry passengers across the ocean.

Her grandmother held great influence over Hancel. She once told her, "You must not sew on Sunday. What you sew on Sunday must be ripped out on Monday, with your teeth. That is a rule my devout Episcopalian mother taught me. Sadie abided by it, and you must do the same. You must keep the Lord's day holy." Her grandmother also frowned on card playing. William liked to play cards with his lodge brothers. After their meetings fellow members often stayed late into the night playing poker. He also smoked a pipe. One night, returning home after a late card session, he knocked the ashes from his pipe, put the pipe in his cardigan pocket, and hung the garment on a peg in the back hallway, before retiring. Some time later the smell of smoke awoke Sadie. Alarmed, she shook William as she called, "William! I smell smoke. Get up! I'm afraid the house is on fire!" He traced the odor to the back hall. A spark from his pipe had ignited the jacket. It was slowly smoldering and soon would have been ablaze. A full can of kerosene, used to start the stove on chilly mornings, sat a few feet away.

When Sadie realized what had caused the near accident, she was angry. "You could have set the entire house on fire with your carelessness!"

"I know. I know. It was foolish of me. I will be more careful in the future." Sadie's mother blamed the whole episode on the card playing and club attendance. William blamed himself. A short time later he made the announcement that he was resigning from his lodge. Sadie questioned him, "Why? I know how much you enjoy an evening out with your friends."

"Yes, but I blame myself for what could have been a tragedy if the house had caught on fire." It became a joke between them that he choose to give up his lodge meetings but did not quite smoking his pipe.

The years passed quickly. Hancel began to take notice of her appearance, and of the clothing she wore. One day she spied a beautiful coat in the local mercantile shop window. It was a great coat that would hang to her ankles; royal blue in color and with gold buttons. She fell in love with it. Each time she passed the window she stopped to admire it. She wanted that coat more than she had ever wanted anything. More than the bonnet she had lost years ago. She thought of the time, long ago, when her grandmother drove the horse and buggy to Logansport to shop. After shopping for groceries, her grandma took her to a dry goods store and bought her a beautiful bonnet. Clusters of tiny pink flowers adorned the brim and a pink ribbon tied under her chin. As they returned home to Monticello, a storm came up. The rain pelted so hard they were forced to seek shelter. They pulled into a farmyard and parked under a roof that connected two corncribs. In the excitement of the storm the new hat was forgotten. When they arrived home the hat was missing. Grandma Paulina said it must have blown off her head during the mad dash. She never forgot that pretty bonnet.

One day she got up enough courage to enter the store and inquire how much the coat cost. She told the storekeeper that she hoped no one bought it, adding, "I'm going to start saving my money. Someday I will buy it. I can earn enough money by picking strawberries and 'tending neighborhood children. I'll do chores until I can buy that coat!"

A few days later, clutching her first savings in her hand, she entered the shop. She asked the owner; "If I pay a quarter every week will you take the coat out of the window and hold it for me until I get it paid for? I'm afraid someone will buy it."

"No. I can't do that. Why don't you run home and ask your father to purchase it for you?"

Several days later the coat disappeared from it's usual place. Hancel was sure it had been sold. She dashed into the store, almost in tears, and asked, "Did you sell the coat? Will you get another one?"

"Now hold on! No, I didn't sell the coat. Since you told me you would save money to buy it, I felt sure you would. Also, it was time to put a new display in the window. I have wrapped the coat and stored it in the stock room. I will hold it for you until you come in to pay for it."

Hancel was so elated she ran all the way home to tell her mother. Sadie asked why she had not asked William to buy the coat for her. She replied that she didn't know why. It was just something in her mind. Since she was the oldest, her father expected more from her than from the others. She just wanted to purchase the coat for herself. Sadie praised her for her self-reliance. Years later, when Hancel related this tale to me she said, "It was a memorable occasion when I was finally able to go in and plunk the money down on the counter and say, 'I've come to pick up the blue coat."

The storeowner said, "I knew you would do it girl. I knew you would do it!"

On her sixteenth birthday William made Hancel a secretary desk. It was made out of cherry wood. One shelf section was enclosed with a long glass door and contained a brass lock and key. One side was topped with a mirror, and a tiny shelf lay above a pigeonhole section. When the door to this section was lowered it became a writing table. The compartment with the lock and key was utilized throughout Hancel's life for filing away important papers, stashing small hoards of cash, ribbon tied bundles of old letters and the family Bible which held recorded dates of births and deaths.

My sister, Little Hancel, still has the old desk. I remember, as we were growing up, the drop down door to the pigeonhole compartment came loose from its hinges. One day, wanting a blackboard on which to do her homework, Hancel removed the door and began using it for a slate. When Mom discovered this she was very irate and ordered Sis never to do it again. But many times, the process was repeated. Sis always said, "I'll use the inside of the door so the marks won't show when the door is closed."

THE YOUNG LADY

With graduation from the eighth grade, Hancel's school days were ended. She matured into a beautiful young lady. Boys began to notice her especially David, a son of old family friends. David's visits with his parents became more appealing, and he accompanied them more often. He began to slick his hair and spruce himself up.

Recreation centered on church activities; the family, box socials, croquet games, and Sunday visits. Soon Hancel and David were pairing off in the parlor. They peered through the stereoscope at visions of Niagara Falls and other far away places. They snatched moments alone for long walks, concerts in the park, and ice cream parlor dates. It was soon accepted that David was Hancel's special beau.

The businessman, from whom Hancel had purchased the coat year ago, expanding his investments, started up the first telephone company in town. Remembering the young girl of the coat episode, now grown into a beautiful young woman, he asked Hancel if she would like to come to work for him as a telephone operator. "You will be trained for the job. It's very simple. Talk it over with your parents and let me know by the end of the week."

Hancel went to work at the phone company, becoming one of the first two operators in town when very few homes had telephones. The work place consisted of a tiny cubical containing a day bed, a small table, and one straight back chair. The switchboard was filled with tiny holes that lit up and flashed when a call was coming in. The operator would insert a plug into the hole with the flashing light, request the number of the party being called, and connect the two parties. Two operators were employed. One worked nights and the other worked during the day. After one month the hours were alternated allowing each girl a change of routine. When she was at work, Hancel could read, embroider or tat, but she always had to remain alert for the flashing lights. She could never allow herself to go to sleep.

Out of habit, David and Hancel drifted into being sweethearts. He bought her a gold ring embossed with two tiny hearts. One heart had a tiny pearl mounted in the center of the heart; the other had a small diamond. The ring implied that someday they would marry. * My sister still has that old ring.

Among the shops located on Main Street was the Golden Eagle Department Store, with an eagle mounted atop a globe of the world sitting in front of the building as it's logo. There was a tobacco store, a man's haberdashery, a drug store with an ice cream parlor, and a millinery shop. There was a tailor shop, shoe and cobblers shop combined, two barbershops, a grocery store, a meat market, a furniture store with an undertaker establishment in the rear of the building, and a café. Located on secondary streets was the bakery, a mercantile store that housed the Masonic Lodge on the second floor. There was blacksmith shop, newspaper and printing office, a hotel, and the phone company located on one of the second floor spaces. Doctor Zimmer's office lay on the corner of Main and Washington Streets, and another doctor conducted business from his home. A creamery was situated on a side street. Besides selling dairy products they sold fresh eggs. Wyandotte and Buff Orphington eggs could be purchased to set in for hatching baby chicks.

Dissecting the town, at intervals, were the three bridges. Across the tracks, at the end of the first bridge, was a grain elevator and another grocery store. Located on Indiana Street, the busiest street in town in those days, were two small factories and, at one time, there were as many as six saloons. There was another hotel, and boarding houses were scattered around town. In keeping with the era there were livery stables, dray companies, hay and straw dealers, and breeders who specialized in selling Belgian and Percheron horses. A wooden corral, usually filled with cattle held for rest, feed, and to be watered before being transported to markets in Chicago, lay along the railroad tracks. The Flint Glass Factory sat between the first and second bridge. In the early days, due to the abundance of wood from the forest, there were many small factories that manufactured barrel staves, railroad ties, picket fencing, churns, and wooden washing machine tubs. All in all, as Hancel was growing up, Upland was a thriving little community that bustled with activities.

HANCEL

LOUIE

Each evening as she walked home from work, Hancel began to notice a handsome young man standing in the vicinity of the café. She assumed he took his meals there. When she passed him, he always smiled, tipped his hat, and murmured "Signora." He was clean-shaven and usually wore black or navy blue trousers, and a white shirt. He always wore a tie and sometimes a suit. Hancel began to look forward to his greetings. She found herself missing him when he was absent.

One day he was not in his usual place, but she spied him walking a short distance ahead. She quickened her pace. She was carrying an umbrella and as she approached him, she transferred the parasol to under her arm, allowing it to protrude frontward. Then, seemingly engrossed in something and not heeding where she was looking, she allowed herself to bump into him jabbing the tip of the umbrella into his back. She apologized for her clumsiness and a conversation ensued. As Hancel said later, "Otherwise he would still be tipping his hat." - Thus my father and my mother met.

Each evening their conversations grew, comments about the weather and idle remarks. She found his accent delightful. She learned that he had emigrated from Caserta, Italy, a small village near Naples, Italy. He arrived at Ellis Island sometime in 1906. She always remembered that it was the same year as the San Francisco earthquake. His name was Louie Benedict. In Italy the name was know as Benedetto.

One day Louie finally got up enough courage to ask if he could walk her home. She let him walk her to the corner near her home. It soon became a daily ritual. However, she never let him walk her all the way home, only to the corner. She didn't know exactly why except she was concerned about what her father's attitude would be. There was David and their understanding. William was happy about their contemplated marriage.

When William learned of her friendship with Louie, he forbade her to see him again, saying, "You shouldn't be involved with anyone except David much less some damn Italian. Isn't a good American boy, with marriage intended, good enough for you?"

Hancel was emotionally confused. She and David had merely drifted into the habit of thinking about marriage. She wondered if he was also having second thoughts. They had both matured during their friendship. One Sunday when David made his usual appearance, she suggested that they go for a walk. Admitting her mental confusion, and mixed emotions, she told David about Louie; and that she believed herself to be in love with him. "I have serious doubts about us getting married. It isn't as if we have made any announcements or finalized our plans. Perhaps we should let the matter rest until I sort out my feelings about Louie. I'll return your ring."

"I gave the ring to you in friendship and affection. Keep it. I would never give it to another. Better we discover now what might prove to be a mistake than later. We can still be friends. I will hold no bad feelings toward you, or toward Louie."

When David did not appear as usual, William asked why. He was adamant that Hancel should cease all contact with Louie. "You're not to see that damn Eye-talian again. That's an order. He's probably a papist, at that."

Hancel continued to let Louie walk her home. They often stopped at the ice cream parlor, or went for a stroll in the park, but she would never let him take her home. When William discovered her persistence in disobeying his order, he delivered an ultimatum. "It's your choice. Either you obey my wishes; desist seeing that man, or you can leave my house. Stay away from that Dago!"

A next-door neighbor, a woman once married to William's brother but now divorced, was Sadie's friend. The children still thought of her as Aunt Lizzy. Hancel went to her in tears. She explained her predicament to Lizzy, who told her, "Bring your young man around for a visit. Before I can intercede, I must judge if he is worthy. If I like him, I will talk to Sadie."

"My mother will never go against my father's wishes, no matter what. She will not help."

Aunt Lizzy liked Louie immediately. He was courteous and mannerly in every respect. He talked of missing his family and the little village where he grew up. His father owned a small farm and vineyard. He had four brothers and a sister, all now living in America. He said he had been very lonesome until meeting Hancel. He related how the family had come to America.

"My Godfather came to America first. He wrote to my father and older brother telling of the opportunities to be found here. My oldest brother immigrated first. His marriage had been arranged months before he departed. He saved passage money for the girl to join him in New York where they were married. Next my father and I came. In time, we saved money and sent for my mother, two younger brothers, and a sister to join us. I have a good job as a glass blower, and have saved my money. I love Hancel and I can offer her a good life."

Lizzy found nothing objectionable with him and tried to convince William. "William, young people in love will do what they will. You should adapt to the situation. You are being stubborn and unjust in your condemnation of Louie." It was to no avail. Escaping an intolerable situation, Hancel soon moved in with Aunt Lizzy.

Louie Benedict & son Joseph

Louie was unhappy with the situation. He received a letter from a friend, a foreman working for the railroad in Greensburg, Ohio. He wrote that if Louie cared to join him, he could assure him of a job. Realizing that this offered an escape from William's dominance, Louie asked Hancel to marry him.

"I love you, Hancel. Marry me and I will write my friend that I will take the job in Ohio. We will leave this town. Time will change your father's feelings. Once we are married, he will change his mind."

When Hancel accepted his proposal, Louie went to talk to William, to seek his permission and his blessing. William was sullen and said he wanted nothing more to do with the matter. Louie politely, but firmly said, "With or without your consent,

Hancel and I intend to get married. Won't you reconsider and give your daughter your blessing?"

William would not relent. Plans proceeded for the wedding. Through letters sent to Greensburg, a job was forthcoming.

Year later, Hancel reminisced about their wedding. "I wore a white, ankle length, linen skirt, and a simple white georgettes blouse with an ivory hand-kerchief linen jabot. I was upset that I had to wear black shoes but they were all I had. Louie wore a blue serge suit. After the ceremony Aunt Lizzy led us into the dining room. The round oak table was covered with a white embroidered cloth and a beautiful wedding cake, which she had baked, sat in the middle of the table. Candlesticks sat on each side of the cake and two tiny rose bowls filled with red velvet roses sat beside the candles. It was a beautiful wedding. Only Aunt Lizzy, her brother, and the minister were present."

"Later, we caught the late train out of town. We went to New York for our honeymoon and to visit Louie's family. He insisted that he had to introduce me to his family. Although I was happy, I was also sad. I had never been away from my family except to visit Grandma Kirk." The year was 1913.

THE SILVER LOVING CUP

The first thing Hancel noticed upon arriving in the big city was the odors and smells; smoke, food aromas, the stench of horse urine rising from the steamy pavement. There were also pleasant aromas of food that created hunger pangs. She could hardly fathom the crowded conditions. The hustle and urban blight of the huge metropolis bore no resemblance to the peaceful serenity, and rustic beauty, of her little hometown. Abusive sounds made her ears ring, the din of the crowds, the clang of the trolley, and the roar of the automobiles. Back home there were only a few cars even though they were being manufactured in Kokomo, a few miles away.

The Benedict's comfortable home was in the Italian section of Astoria. Behind the house was a small woodshed. This was the living quarters for three young men recently arrived from Italy, cousins or related in one degree or another. Louie's father had sponsored them in coming to America. He would assist them in finding jobs in a factory, steel mill, tailor shop, or on the railroad. They were charged no rent for the shed, only for the food that they consumed. Louie's mother cooked pots of stews, soups and pastas. She fried skillets of fish and tons of potatoes. Anything nourishing, inexpensive, and easily prepared was carried out to them. The men brewed pots of coffee over a small brazier that sat in the yard. The shed contained three cots, a small table and three chairs. Sanitary facilities consisted of the outhouse and a washbasin by the pump in the yard. A galvanized tub hung on the side of the shed. Water for an occasional bath was heated over a fire built in a brick pit in the yard. The tub was also used for washing clothes. By the time that winter arrived the men would seek housing elsewhere. In the interim, the arrangement allowed them to save money to establish themselves in Illinois, Indiana, Ohio, and even California where they might find employment.

Louie said, "When we first arrived in America we lived in much the same way. First, Tony's godfather came. Someone had helped him so he helped Tony. Tony helped my father and me."

Hancel often spoke of those days in New York. A chance event, a newspaper item or a familiar song might pry something from the recesses of her mind. Years later when one of her grandchildren asked for school lunch money, she remembered a long ago conversation between two young mothers in New York.

"A new policy is being tested in the public schools. For three cents each, per day, schoolchildren can buy a hot lunch. The Italian school district is trying out the new practice by serving food suited to the Italian palate. In Jewish schools Kosher meats are served, and the Irish children are served no meat on Fridays. Cooks and workers, in most cases the children's mothers, are paid one dollar a day. Older students carried the trays, served the food, and washed the dishes. The mothers are happy with the new plan since it saved them money. Often this meal is the only one poorer pupils have all day."

The newly weds spent a week with the family before leaving for Greensburg, Ohio. Louie reported to work on the railroad. Railroad cars, parked along the rail sidings, served as living quarters, supplied by the company. Married couples were furnished small apartment units consisting of a galley type kitchen and a tiny bedroom. This housing could be moved from town to town as tracks were laid and work expanded. A nominal rent was charged and withheld from workers pay envelope.

Louie was not accustomed to back breaking labor that wore blisters on his hands. Hancel found it hard to adjust to cinders and smoke. After a few weeks they moved to Pittsburgh, Pa. Louie immediately found employment as a glass blower. They rented an apartment on the top floor of a private dwelling. It was more to Hancel's liking and a great improvement over the railroad housing. The landlord and his wife were French people, second generation removed from the old country. Hancel immediately took to Annette, the wife, who was not much older than her. She was, however, several years younger than her husband, Jules?

Louie quickly made friends with fellow workers and fellow countrymen in the Italian community. He joined the Italian Club. Each week dances were held at the club hall. Louie liked to dance and was a graceful dancer. Hancel could not dance well. Having been reared by the strict rules as applied by her Grandmother Kirk, that instilled the notion of dancing being sinful, she found it hard to rid herself of her inhibitions. Try as she would, her feet would not follow where Louie's led. The Italian Club was going to hold a waltz contest as a part of the New Years celebration. A silver loving cup would be awarded to each partner. They need not be husband and wife. They could be brother and sister or merely friends.

Hancel was expecting and in no shape to dance even if she was a good dancer. She mentioned the contest to Annette saying that it was a shame that Louie didn't have a partner to enter the contest with. Annette, who was not much old than Louie, said she would like to enter the contest with him. Jules would not object. He liked Louie, and he also liked for her to have a good time. He didn't like to dance. Hancel told Louie. Annette told Jules. It was agreed that the two would be contestants at the New Years Eve ball. They began to practice in the parlor as Jules and Hancel watched. The big night arrived. Hancel was excited. Louie laughingly said, "Hancel, you are like a prima-donna on grand opening night. One would think you were going to do the dancing."

Jules and Hancel found seats along the wall where they could watch. The band struck up a waltz tune. Couples twirled across the floor, dashing dark men and ladies with elegantly coiffures and beautiful gowns. As the contest progressed, dancing couples were eliminated until only three remained on the floor. Then only two remained. Finally, Louie and Annette received the most applause. The audience kept calling their number. Alone, they once more glided gracefully over the polished floor, dipping and twirling for the pleasure of the onlookers. They won the silver loving cup. For years it sat on a pedestal in our parlor beside a picture of Louie. It was Mom prize possession.

Louie and Loving Cup

JOSEPH AND WILLIAM

In the dark early hours of the morning Hancel lay awake listening to the staccato clop of horses hoofs and the squeak of wood grating against wood as wagons swayed and clattered up the steep hills of the city. The brewery wagons were making their daily deliveries of barrels of beer to the saloons. During the night, after the contents were consumed, the empty barrels were rolled down the hill. By morning many lay stacked in piles for easy pick up. During the day she watched little children carry empty growlers, covered buckets, to the saloon to be filled with beer. A full bucket of beer sold for a nickel.

With trepidation, not knowing if William's animosity still prevailed, Hancel wrote to Sadie. An answer quickly came back with surprising news. Sadie was expecting a baby.

"Another child! I'm too old to be having a baby! I am not happy with the prospect but I have reconciled myself. I learned, years ago, that life is not always happiness. William is too old to be raising another child. He should be looking forward to a little rest not to increasing the population."

Although Hancel was homesick she bubbled over with news when Louie arrived home from work. Louie had also received a letter from his family. His two brothers had moved to Chicago Heights, Illinois. His parents would be moving there soon. A few weeks later Louie suggested that they join the family in the Heights. "With the baby coming, Hancel, it would be good for you to be close to family. Tony's wife, Mary, would be a comfort. The economy is good. I will always find a job. We might as well see what this country is like before we have to settle down.

"We've already moved twice since we were married. We cannot be moving constantly."

"There will be plenty of time for that after the baby arrives."

26

In a few weeks they moved to the Heights. They rented an apartment in the Italian section of the city. The language barrier proved to be a problem for Hancel. The younger ones spoke English but lapsed into their mother tongue when conversing with the older folks. When the family gathered they often forgot that Hancel could not understand them, and was excluded from the discussions. Upon realizing their omission, they immediately switched to English so she could participate.

There were many onion fields in the area, consequently a factory that manufactured onion salt and onion powder. Louie had no trouble securing a job. While he was at work, Hancel joined young nieces in the fields gathering onions. It was stoop labor but she did not mind. It gave her the opportunity to mingle and make friends. She was allowed to set her own hours. She took pride in earning money to buy new things for the expectant infant. After a few weeks Louie made her quit. "Our baby is more important than the money you earn. You must stay at home before some harm comes."

One day an alarm sounded at the factory, indicating that an accident had occurred. Workmen rushed to discover the cause, and to offer assistance. Louie ran to investigate the commotion, but fellow workers held him back. His young brother-in-law had jumped into a vat filled with pulverized onions. He was the first to see the workman struggling in the large vat of dry powder, which sifted and flowed like quicksand. Shouting an alarm, he jumped into the vat in an attempt to rescue the floundering man. The more they struggled, the deeper they sank. Both lost their lives, suffocated under tons of onion salt. It was a devastating blow to his young wife, Julia, left widowed with two small children. It was a tragic loss to the entire family.

Despite family sorrow it was a happy time for Hancel as she busily sewed tiny garments for her first child. What she could not make, she bought, especially Ruben shirts. They were advertised as absolute protection for tiny chests, with double thickness over tummy and lungs to prevent colds and colic; no buttons; just wrap and tie. She would wrap her baby in Ruben shirts. She sent for free pamphlets on childcare issued by the Agriculture Department. Instructions noted that mother's milk would be best for infants, fewer problems with summer complaints.

Their first son, Joseph, was born on August 13, 1914, almost to the day that completion of the Panama Canal was announced. Started by the French, who had long ago given up on the project, it was finished with American ingenuity and will power.

Italian families are closely bonded. They love one another. They rejoice at the birth of a baby, dance at weddings, and sob together to sustain each other in sorrow and death. The birth of Joseph coincided with the arrival the sad message that Louie's grandfather, back in Italy, was in failing health. There was no one to care for him, or attend to the vineyard. Soon Louie's parents would have to return to Italy. There was both joy and sorrow in the family.

Letters began to arrive from overseas. "War is becoming imminent. Archduke Ferdinand, of Austria, was assassinated in Sarajevo. Hardships and discontentment are mounting. I hope Italy will not be entangled in the conflict if war comes, but the situation doesn't look encouraging.

Headlines read: Germany Declares War on Russia. Kaiser Hurls Armies Into Belgium:

The Kaiser's army marched into Belgium, igniting flames of war. Great Britain demanded their withdrawal. When Germany refused, England and Canada declared war on Germany. Italy became involved and soon all Europe was inflamed in war.

The Italian community buzzed with talk of battles and invasions. Every few days an acquaintance from the old country sailed home to fight with Italy's army. Louie's young brother, Mike, received a letter from his father saying, "Your country expects all loyal sons of Italy to come home and fight for their country." Mike felt no compulsion to enter the fray for Italy. He was now an American citizen. He soon enlisted.

Hancel's sister, Vivian, wrote that as a suffragette, she was marching for the right to vote. Her letter noted that the U. S. House of Representatives had rejected the proposal that would allow women that right, but she was confident it would come. "The suffragettes hold Susan B. Anthony as their model. She even dared to vote in one Presidential election. Her ballot was destroyed and she was fined one hundred dollars, but she refused to pay it. Her consensus is that the Constitution of the United States says 'we the people, not we the white male.' With this as our battle cry, and with her as our example, women are fighting for that right." Vivian also wrote that she had met the man she was going to marry, a conductor on the railroad. "He often lays over at the hotel, between runs, so we can get better acquainted. We plan to move to his hometown, Logansport, Indiana, after we are wed."

Louie realized that Hancel was homesick. He knew that factories were running at full capacity due to the war in Europe. They began making plans to return to Upland. He would get his old job back at the Flint glasshouse.

Hancel and her father did not reconcile immediately. He was stubborn. He also was not well. He looked old and tired. Sadie said he would come around in time. Little by little the animosity disappeared.

The factory was in full swing and the town was crowded. Rentals were hard to find. They stayed with Aunt Lizzy until they could find a dwelling. For lack of anything better they inquired about an abandoned house, which the owner had once used as a chicken roost. At the prospect of collecting rent on the building, it was remodeled and rented to them.

War news intensified. Woodrow Wilson was determined to keep the United States free from foreign entanglements. America had enough trouble at home. Poncho Villa and his band of Mexican out-laws raided Columbus, New Mexico shooting up the town and killing several townspeople. The bandits kept John Pershing busy chasing them up and down the border.

Times were changing. The horse and buggy was moving over to make room for the Model T. Henry Ford promised round money for a fair days labor and instituted a new installment plan. One could buy a Ford for three hundred and fifty dollars. They could "ride now and pay later." But many had no faith in the flivver and preferred old Dobbin. School boys chanted: "Henry Ford made a model T. T-Lizzy, T-Lizzy hunk of tin. Rattle! Rattle! Boom boom! Tin! Tin! Tin!"

Hancel was expecting again. When the baby was about due to arrive, she sent word to the glasshouse for Louie to come home. The new baby was a boy. When Louie returned to work the next day he announced to his fellow workers that he had a new son. When they asked what he looked like? Louie answered, "He is long and skinny like the T T bottle." This was a hand blown bottle produced at the factory and used to ship medicine to the battlefront. Thereafter, the men at the factory referred to the boy as little TT.

Thus my brother acquired a nickname that stuck with him throughout his entire life. Fellow classmates, team players, and just plain buddies called him Tee. Some said they didn't know he had any other name. While most called him T, or TT, Hancel called him Willie. Throughout this tale I shall call him Willie.

JULIA

Louie bought a house at the edge of town, where the brick road ended and a gravel road began. It was a two-bedroom house with a family size kitchen, up to date with a porcelain sink and running water. A double, folding parlor door could be closed during the winter to conserve fuel. An entrance hall gave access to either the main living room or the parlor. Gas jets protruded from the plaster walls and natural gas supplied a cheap source of heating fuel. Hancel could push her two boys to town in a wicker baby buggy, or to visit Sadie. An identical house, except for color, sat next door. A newly married couple, Harvey and Emma, occupied it. Emma was expecting her first baby. Hancel, also, was expecting again.

The war escalated as German U-boats cruised dangerously close to America's shores, hampering U.S. vessels. Germany was warned to stay out of U.S. waters. When they announced their policy of unrestricted submarine warfare, America severed all diplomatic relations with them. On April 2, 1917 President Wilson asked Congress to declare war on Germany "to make the World safe for democracy." Four days later, with Congressional approval, a proclamation was signed stating: "A state of war exists between Germany and the United States of America."

The first lottery drafting men into the armed services went into operations. Hancel worried that Louie would be called up. Since they already had two children, and with another on the way, his number would not go into the draft unless the war was prolonged. War news worsened daily. Two ammunition ships collided in Halifax Harbor, Nova Scotia, far from Europe's shores. The exotic Dutch dancer, Mata Hari, was executed before a firing squad as a spy.

Hancel's birth pains occurred during the night. Louie dashed up town to get Dr. Zimmer. Hancel was having a hard

31

labor. When the infant finally did appear the umbilical cord was wrapped around its neck. Removing the cord, the doctor slapped the baby 's bottom trying to force it to cry, to inhale air and start the breathing process. When it did not respond Dr. Zimmer shouted, "Quick, get a glass of cold vater to throw on this child. Ve must shock it in order to make it cry."

In the excitement, and confusing Dr. Zimmer's language, laced with a strong Dutch accent, Louie returned with a glass of coal oil. He splashed it on the baby, as instructed. The baby let out a lusty cry. Dr. Zimmer sniffed the air and demanded, "Vhat did you 'ave in dat glass, I smell kerosene!"

Upon learning that it was indeed kerosene, he bellowed, "I said cold vater not coal oil! Get lard, or oil to rub on this babe." Thus, I, Julia Vivian, entered the world on November 29th, 1917.

Louie was so captivated with his new little daughter he rushed out and purchased a new player piano saying, "When my little girl is big enough she will learn how to play the piano. Until then, my beautiful Hancel, you will play the music rolls. All you do is insert a cylinder and pump the pedals. I bought lovely songs for you to enjoy." Hancel read the titles inscribed on the boxes: Let the Rest of the World Go By; I'm forever Blowing Bubbles; Beautiful Isle of Somewhere, songs of the era, and Louie's favorite song, Santa Lucia.

Emma's baby girl, Paula, was born pathetically under nourished. Dr. Zimmer stopped to see Hancel. He did not ask, he merely instructed her, "Emma had not enough milk to feed her infant. It has been living on barley water and whiskey and what little suck it can get from her Mama. You will nurse Emma's baby along with yours. Drink lots of milk and eat wholesome foods." He did not doubt that Hancel would comply. In those days, it was customary for women to wet-nurse another's infant.

Louie bought Hancel a new Globe kitchen range. It was black and shiny with nickel trim. It had four burners, an oven, and an overhead warming oven. The water reservoir kept a supply of hot water always ready. Hancel kept the stove blackened and the nickel gleaming by buffing it with cheesecloth. "She caresses it" as Louie said. He was amused at the attention she gave her prize possession.

Hancel often recited the story of the first time she cleaned the accumulated soot from the catch box. As she wondered, aloud, how and where to dispose of the soot, Louie said, "Why, Hancel, don't you know if you take that soot up to the hardware store they will pay you ten cents a pound for it. The government buys it to use in making explosives for the war."

Having perfect faith in her husband, Hancel packaged up the soot. The next day she put her children in the buggy and walked to the hardware. She told the proprietor, "I have a bag of soot to sell."

The puzzled storeowner asked, "You have a bag of what to sell?"

"I have a bag of soot from the kitchen range trap. Louie says you buy it to sell to the government to be used in making explosives."

With amusement, the man said, "Hancel, I'm afraid Louie is playing a joke on you. I don't buy soot, and I'm sure the government doesn't either." Although embarrassed, Hancel laughed along with Louie when he learned she had been gullible enough to try to sell the soot.

Because of the war austere measures were taken to conserve food. Meatless and wheatless days were instituted as a method of saving food. Anyone eating meat or bread on those days was considered unpatriotic. As a part of the war effort, and to reserve staples for the fighting men, bakers asked their customers to place bread orders a day ahead of their pick-up date, to order sparingly and only in necessary quantities so bread wouldn't be wasted and flour would be saved. With the demand for troop trains the government ordered railroads to double up on freight shipments. All cloth and leather went to clothe the army. It was impossible for a civilian to buy a pair of shoes.

Hancel's brother, Jay enlisted in the Navy. Letters were few and far between, and his whereabouts unknown. Newspapers printed heroic tales of how Sergeant Alvin York, in the Battle of the Argonne Forest, killed and captured several German soldiers. On the home front, people were dying by the thousand in a great flu epidemic. Supposedly, soldiers at an army camp in the states were the first to contact the disease. It quickly spread to other camps and troops, aboard ship, transported it to Europe causing the epidemic to engulf the world. In those days there were no miracle drugs, no antibiotics to combat the scourge, people relied mostly on antiquated old home remedies.

MINNIE

Shortly after the war ended Sadie received a letter. It was postmarked Monticello, Indiana. The letter stated: "I think I am your sister." It was signed Minerva S. Moore. Sadie knew from the letters contents that the writer must, indeed, be her sister. Through a steady flow of letters, arrangements were made for the two sisters to meet at the train station in Logansport. Sadie rode the train from Upland and Minerva, or Minnie as she became known, arrived by horse and buggy from Monticello. By the time the reunion took place both sisters were over fifty years of age. Minerva had lost a son killed in World War 1. The following story is as I remember hearing it many times during my childhood.

In the early pioneer days two Kirk brothers migrated from Scotland, where the name meant a wee church. They settled in North Carolina. Later one crossed the Cumberland Gap and settled in Indiana. Through the years, letters described the journey and how the brother had built a cabin in the wilderness. The tales always intrigued a young nephew, Andrew Kirk.

When Andrew grew up he fought as a Union soldier during the Civil War. Upon returning home from the war he found his home destroyed and life, as he knew it before the war, forever changed. His in-laws, and neighbors, could not forgive him for having fought with the Yankees. As a veteran he was entitled to file for homestead land. He decided to take his wife and little daughter and go to Indiana, perhaps on to Iowa. They would start a new life.

Andrew wrote to his uncle, who encouraged them to join him. Andrew built a covered wagon to be used as transportation and also to house them until they were established wherever they settled. Following the same route the uncle traveled, years ago, their journey began in 1870.

35

When they arrived in Cincinnati, Ohio they stopped in a respite area where travelers heading west could stop to rest. They stayed for several weeks while Andrew worked at a blacksmith shop in order to augment their meager savings. When they continued their journey, somehow the little daughter became separated from the family and was lost. For days they searched, fruitlessly, before being forced to resume their journey.

According to the tale, the father later retraced their trail to Cincinnati in hopes of discovering information about the lost child. Although the trip proved futile he returned with tales of crime and corruption that prevailed in the city. He told how gambling establishments flourished, often two and three in a row; the Sun Saloon near the fountain; the Empire Saloon on Race Street: two side by side on Vine Street and two more down the street. All had Keno rooms and poker parlors. Chuck-a-luck and roulette were played nightly, also a French game called Rough-et-noir. Decoys lured men into these dens of iniquities. The goose, where players picked up their winnings, remained open day and night. Cunning shill men circulated about inveigling hapless winners into more games. Unscrupulous politicians controlled the city, and frequented these houses.

He also so reported that a religious revival was sweeping the country. The Methodist Church, once torn apart by slavery, had reunited as the Methodist Protestant Church. He added, "The Civil war is still being fought, verbally, all over the South."

These tales were repeated to me as having been told to Hancel by her grandmother Kirk. Her grandmother also told her that, as a young girl, she attended camp meetings in the woods at a place called Battleground. The stories were probably about Grandma Kirk's second husband's family. None reveal how Minnie was lost. Articles discovered in an old newspaper, pages from the Cincinnati Weekly Gazette dated 1876, confirm the facts about the city of Cincinnati. It was discovered tucked away in a box of old books of Hancel's, probably acquired from her Grandma.

Kirk, and saved through the years.

Also found among the old papers and books was a copy of a Grand Army of the Republic booklet, dated 1888, issued at a meeting in Indianapolis. At that meeting the custom of lowering the flag to half-mast on Memorial Day, in honor of fallen companions, was established.

The name Kirk was carried on through Hancel's second son, William Kirk Benedict. Her son Joseph's middle name is Andrew.

THE LITTLE FARM

Gradually, one visit at a time, William and Louie reconciled. At least they tolerated each other. Hancel never knew the exact moment when tolerance changed to acceptance but gradually a mutual respect developed. She also knew that her father was ill. He lacked interest in projects that once engrossed him. He coughed often and ran a fever daily. At Sadie's insistence he finally went to the doctor. The diagnosis was consumption, as tuberculosis was called in those days. He could not support his family. They fell on hard times.

Aunt Vivian, usually referred to as "Vi", was married and lived in Logansport. Only one young daughter remained at home. Someone had to earn a living. Vi suggested that Sadie and her daughter come live with her family. Sadie could find work as a domestic. William, unable to contest the situation, was forced to agree. Sadie did what she had to do.

Louie offered to let William stay with them until Sadie was settled and more secure. This would enable him to avoid the temptation to plunge himself into work. He needed rest. A room was added to their home, thus allowing William privacy. At Dr. Zimmer's suggestion, crank out windows were installed near the ceilings to allow lots of fresh air into the room. It was believed that cold air retarded the illness. A side window allowed William to lie in bed and gaze out the window. A door opening into the main room allowed Hancel to bring in meals, away from the children. A washstand and lava bowl served for hygienic purposes, and a chamber pot sat under the bed, and one could exit an outside door to the path leading to the privy.

When the time came for William to take his place in Louie's household, he said, "Louie, I cannot stay with you until I admit I was wrong in my intolerance, my prejudice of you being Italian. I was a bigot."

"It is of no importance. It shall never be mentioned between us."

Aunt Vi opened a café in Idaville.

One evening, as Louie sat on the front porch, a neighbor stopped to visit. The man mentioned that he was going to sell his house and five acres of land and purchase a home closer to town.

"Five acres of land, you say? I might be interested in that."

Yes, five acres of land with the house, a little barn, and a couple of chicken houses. The house has a front parlor, a big kitchen, two bedrooms, and a lean-to-add on room that can be used as a third bedroom. It also has a big room we use as a store room."

Louie had always dreamed of owning a small farm. For days he thought about the prospects of buying the property. He finally discussed the subject with Hancel, who wasn't pleased with the idea of leaving her new home. She also wondered where they would get the money.

"I have some savings, and we can rent this house to help pay for the other. If you find you're not happy, we can always move back here. It would be a good investment."

The seller agreed to accept the player piano as a down payment and hold a contract for the balance. Payments would be made quarterly. When Hancel learned the player piano would be used to secure the property, she reminded her husband of his plans for Julia to learn to play the instrument someday. He laughingly promised to buy another one when she was old enough. The sale was concluded.

The move to the little farm meant more work for both of them. After toiling all day in the glasshouse, Louie would come home and plow the land, till the soil, and plant crops. He even prepared a vegetable plot for Hancel. He bought a wagon and a horse named Dolly.

There was no running water in the house. A cistern was located outside the back door. A filled bucket of water, with a dipper floating in it, always sat on the dry sink cabinet. In the fall they picked pears from two trees. Wrapped in paper and packed in a barrel, to ripen slowly, they were sweet and succulent when ripe and ready for eating.

Hancel grew fresh vegetables. Those not consumed immediately where packed into jars for use during the winter. In the fall Louie dug a deep pit and filled it with straw. He layered turnips, cabbage, carrots, potatoes, and apples between layers of straw, and heaped soil over them, creating a huge mounded root cellar. In the spring, when this root cellar was opened, the vegetables supplied nourishing food for the table until a new crop could be raised and harvested. They raised chickens for fresh eggs, and many ended up in the skillet or stew pot.

Hancel often mentioned Louie's first melon patch. His little son, Joseph, loved to help tend the melons, weeding and watering them. Together, father and son watched them grow, waiting for them to mature. One day when Louie arrived home from work Joseph ran across the field to meet him. He eagerly led his father to the melon patch. At the edge of the garden, laid out in neat rows, was the entire crop of melons; big ones and little ones; ripe ones and half grown green ones. Needless to say, there weren't many melons harvested that year.

The Pennsylvania Railroad tracks ran parallel, and behind their property line. Louie could walk across his field, crawl through the fence, and walk the switch track to the glass factory. As he walked to work, he savored the satisfaction of owning his own land, and life center around his family. Life was good. He was at peace.

It soon became a time of peace throughout the world. It was a time for rejoicing. On the eleventh day of the eleventh month, at the eleventh hour, November 11, 1919 the war ended. Peace agreements were signed. The soldiers would be coming home. Louie's brother, Mike, would be one of them. With his parents back in Italy there was no home for him to return to. Louie wrote and invited him to stay with them for a while. He could make his home with them while he rested and decided what to do with his life.

By the end of 1919 thousands of doughboys, who had fought the war to end all wars, came home. Bands played as they marched in parades in New York City and hometowns all over the United States.

UNCLE MIKE

Clad in a khaki colored uniform, with leggings wrapped to his knees, and a knapsack on his back, Uncle Mike returned home. At first all he wanted to do was rest his body and mind. He was not a big man. He was only five foot- five inches tall. But to me he was taller than Maypole. He had brown curly hair and he rolled his own cigarettes.

In the evenings, after supper was over and Louie's chores were done, we would sit outside and listen to Uncle Mike recite tales of his war adventures. If the air was chilly he wrapped me in his army blanket. I hated the blanket. It was scratchy and made me itch, but I wouldn't tell him for fear that he would not hold me. After wrapping the cover around me he pinned it shut with a huge army issue safety pin, which he said he had used to pin captured Germen soldiers together by their noses. When he ran out of tales he sang songs like:

"Kaiser Bill went up the hill to take a look at France.
Kaiser Bill came down the hill with a load of bullets in his pants
Or— How you gonna keep em down on the farm after they've seen Paree?
"How you gonna keep 'em away from Broadway ——
Paintin' the town— Jazzing around."

The rhythm of the songs, the drone of voices in conversation, the sounds of crickets and cicadas, and the gentle rustle of the leaves would soon lull me to sleep.

Too quickly it was time for Uncle Mike to think about employment. He opened a one-chair barbershop. In a short time he expanded to three. Next door to the barbershop was a millinery shop. It was owned and operated by a young lady whose beauty and physical attributes he extolled daily. Her name was Maudie. She boasted of being Cincinnati trained in the art of attaching buttons and bows on straw hats and felt hats. As a Suffragette, who had marched for the right to vote, she was emancipated. She espoused Women's Lib long before the phrase was coined. Maudie became my aunt.

While there were a few Tin Lizzys around town, our mode of transportation was still a wagon pulled by old Dolly. On Sunday Hancel often packed a lunch and we would drive to the park for a picnic. Since the park was only a short distance to Uncle Mike's and Aunt Maudie's house, we often drove over for a visit. One Sunday we arrived to find Uncle Mike covered with soot. Black powdery film was sprinkled all over the floor and the contents of the room. Aunt Maudie was very irate, verbally so. Uncle Mike was no less agitated. He saw no need in taking down the parlor stove, storing it in the shed for the summer months, and putting it up again when winter arrived. He also knew, before he started, that it was not a one-man job. At Maudie's insistence, he had undertaken the task. Louie helped complete the chore, after which we made a hasty departure.

Louie bought us a little wagon with a bench seat for the driver and an open carrying bed. The wagon was painted green and was trimmed in gold just like his big wagon. We had a pet goat named Billy. With Billy hitched to the wagon, we rode up and down the road, around the yard and through the empty fields. My brothers always sat on the seat. They took turns holding the reins and steering the wagon. I was never allowed to sit on the seat or drive Billy. I was always relegated to the wagon bed.

Hancel was expecting again. With so much work to do, she wondered how she would manage with another infant. But life was good. They even managed to hoard a little money now and then. She filled glass jars with vegetables, stuffed peppers with cabbage and packed them down in crocks. Emma and Paula visited almost daily. They helped shell peas and green beans and usually carried something home to temp Paula's appetite in order to fatten her frail body. It was apparent that her vision was impaired. She constantly stumbled and bumped into objects. When peering at something, she held it close to her face.

Life was changing in America. Prohibition became the law of the land. Bootleggers appeared on the scene. Bootlegger was a term coined in Scotland when a tax was levied on whiskey. Smugglers tucked bottles of booze inside their boot to smuggle it past tax collectors. To the bootleggers of the twenties that was penny-anti stuff. They smuggled it by the barrel, in boats, and by the truckloads.

The twenties produced the term speak-easy. Illegal brew could be bought by merely whispering, to a guard on the door, "Charlie sent me." Whatever it was called, Speak-easy or Hooch-haunt, liquor flowed freely as police often looked the other way. Palms were greased and bribes paid as business flourished.

Prohibition created gangsters like Al Capone, known in Italian communities as the second-hand furniture man. He staked out a territory and controlled it with petty henchmen and tough hoodlums. Booze paved the way for a sexual revolution. Sex in the back seat of a car while parked in a dark country lane paraphrased the catchword Lover's Lane.

It also ushered in Anti-Saloon Leagues. Although Carrie Nations, known for zeal in battling Demon Rum by busting up booze joints, smashing bottles and mirrors, and in the process whacking a bartender now and then, was dead her avid followers had taken up the hatchet. Know as the Woman's Christian Temperance Union, they preached abstinence and exhorted pledge signings. Prohibition lasted for thirteen years. It has been referred to as "a failure and an experiment noble in purpose." It ushered in an age of decadence, loose morals, and an era like none other; "The Roaring Twenties."

The Twenties also saw a revival of the Ku Klux Klan. After the Civil War, young southern gentlemen organized to protect their property against carpetbaggers and marauding slaves. They dressed in white robes, hid behind masks, and conducted secret raids. After being dormant for years a Methodist preacher, in Atlanta, Georgia led a group of white supremacists to the top of Stone Mountain, burned a cross and revived the Klan.

The Klan spread hatred against the Jews, Catholics, the Irish and especially Blacks. They battled the Sons of Italy and the Knights of Columbus. Klan members were white Protestants and considered themselves Christian. By 1919 and 1920 they began to march again. In Indiana they enrolled new members, increased their ranks, and involved themselves in politics.

Hancel and Louie's lives continued as usual. It was not that they were not interested in what transpired outside their lamplight, but they were content with life. Hancel was occupied with her home and her children, and Louie tended his land. They let the rest of the world roll by.

Every afternoon as Joseph walked home from school two neighbor boys constantly harassed him. He was afraid of them and often came home in tears. He told his father that Willard and Wilbur Worm (fictious names) tease him and call him names.

"What do they call you?"

"They call me Dago."

"Are you sure you don't do anything to incite them into doing so?"

"No, I don't do anything. They just pick on me."

"Just ignore them. They will soon tire of it."

The next day Louie watched Joseph back down the road with the Worm boys in pursuit, pelting rocks at him. He took Joseph aside and told him, "Son, you must learn to fight back. You must not let those boys intimidate you or they will persist in bullying you. If I see you back down that road, away from them, one more time, I shall have to whip you."

The next day Joseph dashed into the yard. He ran to the pear tree and filled his cap with hard green pears and piled them beside the road. Soon the neighbor boys came sauntering by. Spying Joseph, they began hooting and calling him names. Joseph selected a pear and pitched it at Wilbur, but missed. This made his tormentors more derisive. Their taunts increased. Joseph picked up another pear and flung it with all his might. It hit Willard squarely in the eye. He yelled, "Just you wait! We'll get you tomorrow!"

The next day Joseph hurried home, prepared his pile of missiles, and waited. This time, after hitting both boys, he ran into the road and started swinging his fists, shouting, "I won't back down from you anymore! Don't call me Dago again!" The bullies fled home threatening to tell their father.

Soon, Mr. Worm appeared. "Louie, what's gotten into that boy of yours? Why did he hit my sons with rocks?

"It wasn't rocks. He hit them with green pears. It's my fault. Your sons have been calling him Dago, and threatening him. I told my Joe that if he backed away from them one more time I would whip him. I'm not ashamed of being a Dago, if that's what I'm called just because I happen to have come from Italy. No son of mine will be ashamed either. Neither shall he let himself be bullied, if I can help it."

Mr. Worm's attitude changed immediately. "I'll have a talk with my boys. During the war I had names hurled at me because I was of German origin. If I hear those sons of mine have been tormenting Joseph again, I'll fan their britches."

Hancel and Louie's fourth child arrived. It was another boy. They named him Louis, after his father.

Once a week, during the summer, my two older brothers and I took turns walking across the field to meet our father as he returned home from work. We were always cautioned to go no farther that the property line; never climb over the railing; and don't you dare go near the tracks.

I can still visualize those walks through the meadow; bees buzzing; wild roses growing along the fencerow; and tiny hummingbirds fluttering around the trumpet vines. I chased butterflies and picked sweet clover to chew on. Sometimes I merely stood and watched the blinking signal lights that lay along the switch tracks while waiting for my father to appear. On hot days he usually brought me a strawberry ice-cream-cone wrapped in tissue thin paper. The cone would be dripping but nothing has ever tasted so good since.

Louie could read very little English but he could calculate sums without a paper and pencil. Hancel wrote letters for him, and nieces answered them for their parents. Their letters expressed concerns about the criminal element, from Chicago, that was infiltrating Cicero and Chicago Heights. How they entices young men into a life of crime with the prospects of easy money, flashy cars, and beautiful girls, thus making it hard for them to resist temptation.

"The bad easily influence the good. It's so sorrowful to hear the lament of friends whose sons have been led into corruption. Sadder yet, for parents who have lost sons to death in gang warfare. We keep our sons involved in church activities, and tell them to be careful in choosing friends. They spend a lot of time at the YMCA gym. Dominic is becoming an excellent boxer and has won several Golden Glove awards. He is going to study to be a barber."

The next letter bore the sad news that their third son, nearing his twenty-first birthday, had been killed. "Last Saturday evening as Joseph walked to the corner drug store, to buy a package of Victrola needles, a car filled with gangsters drove by. As they opened fire on a rival gang's car machine gun bullets struck our Joseph in the neck. He was killed instantly. He died before a priest could arrive to administer the last sacraments. We are all heartbroken. Ma wants to move away from the Heights before anything else happens." A few weeks later news arrived. "We have moved to Indianapolis. Pa is working for the railroad. Brother Frank has opened a fruit and vegetable store on Washington Street. Ma seems much happier here."

THE GOOD LIFE

Louie liked to get dressed up and walk up town. Perhaps meet with a few cronies for a game of cards, or merely sit on a bench and talk. When the new movie house came to town he took turns taking my brothers and me to the movies. At such times, after he shaved and put on a freshly ironed shirt, it was my job to go to his dresser, take down a long hand carved wooden box, remove a clean white handkerchief from it and bring it to him. He always exuded a scent of cologne or after-shave lotion.

Hancel had just bought me a new red cape with an attached hood. The first time I wore it was to accompany Dad to the new movie theater. He tied my hood ribbon under my chin and said he was going to show me off to his friends. Holding tightly to his hand, I walked proudly beside him on my way to attend my first movie.

Most evenings he spent performing numerous tasks around the little farm. He considered this therapy, an unwinding and release of tension from the daily confines of the glass factory. After completing his chores, and washing up at the pump, he would call, "Hancel come sit with me, rest a bit." With his chair tilted back against the house, he would reach in his shirt pocket for a package of cigarette papers and a bag of tobacco. Holding the tiny square of paper between his thumb and forefinger, he tamped tobacco from the cloth bag onto the paper. He then inserted the drawstring, with attached tag, between his teeth, gave a tug to close the bag and returned it to his pocket. He smoothed the tobacco over the paper, licked the paper and sealed the cigarette by twisting the ends. A match was ignited by rubbing it along the side of his pants, or by snapping off the tip with his fingernail. He was now ready to talk to Hancel about current events, and mundane subjects, as they watched their children. It was the best part of the day.

He bought an old sow pig. It soon produced a litter of piglets. Funny little pink creatures, with curly tails, that squealed and scurried in their pen. I loved to watch them and ached to hold one. Somehow, I managed to crawl from a hole in the barn into the pigsty. When I finally caught one of the baby pigs it squealed in fright and brought the old sow down on me with a vengeance. Louie leaped over the fence and rescued me. He swore he would get rid of the sow, and the piglets, too, unless I promised never to go near the pen again.

The piglets grew and were soon sold. The old sow was butchered. As Louie eviscerated the pig he washed and cleaned the bladder. He inserted a hollow reed into it and created a balloon. We took turns playing with it until Hancel discovered "the filthy thing" and destroyed it. Toys for Tot were hard to come by in those days. You made playthings out of whatever was available.

The meat was rubbed with salt, sage and spices, wrapped in cheesecloth and packed in wooden barrels. Hams were hung from rafters in the smoke house to be cured. Fat was rendered into lard by cooking it in a huge black pot hung over a fire in a backyard pit. We snacked on crisp crunchy cracklings and Hancel baked crackling cakes. Fried sausage patties were packed into tin cans, covered with hot melted lard, and the cans were sealed with sealing wax.

More and more men joined the Klavens of the Klan. They selected fancy names like the Grand Dragon, Grand Cyclops, and Grand Wizard. They began to dominated politics and political leaders in Indiana. They advocated that only native-born Americans should be allowed in the government -and they didn't mean the Indians!

Little playmates bragged about belonging to the Kiddy Klan. Proud mothers, who called themselves Ladies of the Invisible Eye, spurred them on. They wrapped them in sheets until all that was visible were the eyes. These little figures, resembling miniature phantoms, lined up at church on Sundays and babbled little ditties; words that held no significances except to other Klan Kiddies. —Dagos didn't belong!

A letter from Italy brought the sad news that Louie's father had died. Louie's mother wanted to return to America. "Things do not bode well in Italy. Signor Benito Mussolini and his Black Shirts are fermenting dissension and civil disturbances. Italy is becoming a Fascist state." She asked her sons to each contribute funds for her passage to California so she could spend her remaining days with her daughter. Her dutiful sons wrote that she should make her plans. Each would pay a share.

President Harding dedicated the tomb of the Unknown Soldier. The Model A Ford was the best selling automobile, surpassing the Chevy and the Hudson. Rudolph Valentino traveled to Crown Point, Indiana, a popular marriage mill of the days, and got married. Crystal sets made their appearance. Next came the radio. Although it would be several years before every home had a radio, slogans began to blare forth-advertising products. Neighborhood kids imitated old time barkers as they ballyhooed phrases like "always a bridesmaid but never a bride." Juicy Fruit Gum boasted of sixteen flavors, and Bran flakes claimed an ounce of prevention was worth a pound of cure."

While life was good, it was saddened by the news that William, Hancel's father had died. After years of battling TB, he died of carcinoma of the stomach. The year was 1922. I remember the dress I wore. Or, perhaps it's because a group picture, taken the day of his funeral, hangs on my wall. It shows Sadie, Aunt Vivian and a small daughter, Hancel, myself; baby Louis, and Aunt Dorothy.

The first natural gas wells discovered in Indiana, in 1888, were in Fairmount, Indiana. Old timers boasted that Upland's came in at a close second and was struck at a depth of nine hundred feet. It produced as much as five million cubic feet of gas daily, the largest capacity in the state. New wells came in almost weekly. Gas was so cheap the average home could be heated for as little as four dollars to as much as twelve dollars per year. Widows were granted half price and churches were heated free of charge. Factories were offered free gas, and even free land to locate in Upland. Upland became a boomtown.

Within a few years gas, that had once been abundant, was played out. Much of it had been wasted. With the loss of cheap energy to operate, factories closed their doors. By the early twenties the Flint Glass Factory ceased productions.

Emma and Harvey were moving to Muncie, Indiana. Harvey had found employment as a carpenter and painter in another glass factory. They would rent their house in Upland and rent another in Muncie. Emma offered to board and room Louie if he decided to seek work in Muncie, an arrangement that would benefit both parties financially. Hancel was expecting again, and Louie would make no move until after the baby arrived.

One bright May morning Hancel sent my two brothers down the street with a note for a neighbor lady. She came rushing in and sent me outside to play. As Dr. Zimmer's car pulled up in front of the house Louie jumped out and dashed inside. Dr. Zimmer slowly got out of the car and strolled up the path. He paused a moment, patted me on the head and said, "I have a little baby in this satchel. If you stay out here and play, like a good girl, I will leave it for you to play with."

"Is it a girl baby or a boy baby? We have enough boys at our house."

"It is going to be a surprise. You will have to wait and see."

It was a girl. I had a little sister. She was named Hancel after her mother.

When Hancel was up and around Louie said, "As soon as you feel that I can do so, I will look for work in Muncie. Although this place is almost paid for, I can never support our family with it alone. We may have to consider selling both places. When I find employment, I will board with Emma and Harvey."

A few weeks later, having found a job, Louie moved in with them in Muncie. He came home on weekends often. He decided to keep the horse and wagon and Billy the goat. Joseph could tend to them. When he suggested getting rid of the chickens, Hancel would not hear of it, saying, "I'll keep the chickens. I like having fresh eggs and chickens for our meals. I just read of a new supplement that makes prolific layers out of sluggish hens. It's a pill called the Ditto Egg Tablet. You just put one in the watering jar and the hens lay more eggs." Louie laughed, but the next time he came home he brought two boxes of pills. They cost fifty cents per box.

At Christmas he came home laded down with packages. He brought me a new doll, a Miss Rosy Cheeks. It had real hair, opened and closed her eyes, said Mama. Shortly after Christmas the doll disappeared. When I finally found it the beautiful hair was gone and she had a hole in the top of her head. My brothers had torn it apart trying to discover what made it open and close it's eyes. Sever weather prevented Louie from coming home for several weeks.

SAD NEWS ARRIVES

My brothers and I were playing in the storeroom, which was also used as our playroom. Using potatoes from the storage basket we were rolling them across the floor for Louis to retrieve. Although he was able to toddle he was still clumsy on his feet. His repeated falls sent us into peals of laughter. It was then that we endowed him with the nickname, Bounce, which has clung to him all his life. Absorbed in our merriment, we did not hear company arrive. When we finally became aware of voices we ran to the kitchen and found Hancel sobbing as Emma tried to console her. She had brought the sad news that Louie was dead, dead at age thirty-eight. Hancel was widowed at twenty-seven years of age, with five small children to rear. Joseph was ten; Willie eight; I, Julia, was six; Louis was two, and the baby, Hancel, was ten months old. It was Sunday March 23, 1923.

Emma said they had all gone to church that morning. Dinner was barely over when Louie complained of having a headache and perhaps a bit of indigestion. He lay down on the floor hoping to ease the pain. Within a few moments he was dead. There was not even time to send for a doctor. When one did arrive he said Louie had died of a cerebral hemorrhage. He also said it was a hazard of the trade of glassblowers.

In those days death was announced by draping a crepe, a black ribbon, on the front door of the deceased's home. This was also an invitation for friends and neighbors to assemble to offer condolences, prayers, and assistance. Funeral parlors were unheard of. The deceased lay in their own home until time to be taken to the church for services, or to the cemetery.

I remember going into the front parlor where my father lay. I thought he had a new bed. It was too high for me to climb up in, to lie beside him as I often did on early mornings. I pushed a chair up close and was trying to awaken him as Aunt Vi entered the room.

I couldn't understand why everyone was crying. Why did they take away the new bed? Where had my father gone? The man whom I knew as the furniture store man, actually the undertaker, carried me out to the car. It was the biggest car I had ever seen. I had never ridden in a car and thought it a great adventure. But everyone was crying. I did not understand it then, but I will never forget that long ride to the cemetery.

Hancel could not fathom how she would raise five children alone. The first suggestion came from Aunt Vi.

"Sell this place and move back to your other house."

"I can't sell it. Louie loved this little farm."

"Yes, but he is no longer here to maintain it. It will be too much work for a woman alone."

"I can't think of that now. I will need the rent from the other house. Thank God the land contract will soon be paid off. I wouldn't even know what price to ask for this place. People are moving to the cities to find employment, just as Louie did. Property values have declined."

It was a sad parting between the two sisters when it was time for Aunt VI to depart. She promised to visit once a month since she had a railroad pass.

Checking Louie's bankbook, Hancel found it showed a balance of a few hundred dollars. It was drawing four per-cent interests. She would not touch a penny until she absolutely had to. The money from his insurance policy would go to pay his funeral expenses and to pay his share of his mother's passage to America. His brothers would protest but it was a promises Louie had made, and as such was an obligation she would fulfill.

Her mind spun in torment. It whirled with plots and mental calculations, "Beef is six cents a pound. Two pounds of coffee cost fifty-five cents. I will use tea it is cheaper. Twenty-seven cents buys three loaves of bread. I still have meat and canned sausage. The lard it's packed in can be used for baking. Why am I trying to figure costs? How in the world am I going to manage? I must find a way to make a living. Something I can do at home as I tend my children.

Her mind would not stop. "I pay twenty-cents for a bar of P and G soap. Fels Naphtha smells better, so clean and fresh. That's it! I can take in washings. I will do whatever I must to support my kids." The baby's cry interrupted her thoughts. It was a long lonely night. Hancel knew that many more disturbing nights would follow.

It was probably ten days, at the most two weeks, after the funeral that a neighbor, old Grandpa Wilson, came calling. Grandpa in name only, a title bestowed as a sign of respect to an older person. Answering the knock on the door, Hancel invited him in. After a few introductory remarks he asked, "Hancel, what are you going to do with that old mare you have? Now that Louie is gone you surely don't intend to keep her, do you?"

"I haven't thought about it. Louie thought he might sell Dolly, and the wagon too, if we had to move away."

Well, that old horse is just going to cost you money, especially if you don't work her. If you want me to take her off your hands, I'll buy her from you," Struggling to hold back the tears, Hancel said, "I don't know if I should sell Dolly. I've had too many things to consider without worrying about that."

"Well, it's something you should study real hard. You know that horse is getting old. If she should up and die on you, you would have to pay to have her hauled to the bone factory."

"What do you mean, the bone factory?"

"Well, if that horse dies you would have to get rid of the carcass. You couldn't bury an animal that size. The bone factory would buy the carcass to make fertilizer, and they'd charge to haul it away." Seeing Hancel's distress, he added, "I tell you what I'll do. Seeing as how you're a poor widow woman with a bunch of kids to raise, I'll give you two dollars for that animal, right here and now."

"No! I have to think about it." Grandpa Wilson prepared to leave, mumbling to himself. As he went out the door he called, "I'll be back. You think it over and you'll see the sense of it."

Hancel had something else to fret about. "It's true the horse is getting old. The oats are almost gone so is the hay, and the corn won't last much longer. If I hire someone to plant the ground on shares, or rent out the land, I won't need the horse. I might as well sell her. I'll have to think about it sooner or later." Her night was filled with dreams, accompanied by the noise of a horse whinnying. She dreamed about a pile of bones with Dolly's head protruding from its midst.

In a few days Grandpa Wilson returned. "Hancel, I tell you what I'll do. I'll pay you three dollars for that horse right now." After the horrible dream of the pile of bones Hancel took the three dollars.

When Joseph saw the horse being led from the barn he ran in the house and asked, "Why is Grandpa Wilson taking Dolly away?" When he learned that he horse had been sold he ran into the barn and hid. When he did not come in at suppertime, Willie was sent to fetch him. He refused to come in. She heard him creep into the house as she was putting Louis to bed. He moped for days, refusing to talk to her.

When Aunt Vi arrived for her next visit, Hancel related the tale of the sale of the horse. When she finished her recitation Aunt Vi slipped on her coat and dashed out the door, banging it behind her, as she called, "Well! We'll just see about his generosity! That old skinflint!"

Retuning a short time later she tossed seven dollars onto the kitchen table, as she laughingly told Hancel, "I gave that old reprobate a piece of my mind. Cheating you like he did and claiming it was generosity! I told him that horse was worth ten dollars if it was worth a penny and I wouldn't leave until he forked over another seven dollars. He hemmed and hawed. I threatened to go to church tonight, as I knew he would, being the good Christian that he is! I said I would stand right up and denounce him, loud and clear, as a hypocrite that cheated a poor widow woman."

"Vi! You didn't!"

"Yes I did. And I meant every word of it! His wife told him, 'Now, Mr. Wilson, you pay that woman what she says, right now.' I don't know if she was afraid I'd expose him at church, or if she was ashamed of him. I just grabbed the money and ran!"

"Oh, Vi, I don't know if I should laugh or cry. I wish I had some of your spunk. That seven dollars will buy a lot of food for my kids."

AN OFFER OF HELP

A few days later a horse and carriage stopped in front of our house. Four gentlemen, wearing black suits and broad brimmed black hats, descended from the vehicle and walked up the path to the house. When Hancel opened the door they introduced themselves as a delegation from the church, from the Quarterly Meeting. They wanted to talk to her as a member of the church. Hancel invited them in and sent us to the playroom.

The spokesman, speaking on behalf of the entire group, offered condolences for the death of her husband, saying, "We did not know thy husband, personally, but we have heard him praised as a good husband and father. I understand he was a Catholic but joined our church since there was none of his faith in town, and he wanted his children reared with a religious background."

Following an acknowledgement from Hancel, they continued, "We are here to offer any assistance thee might need. It is our church policy to help our families in distress."

"I want no charity. I'll manage somehow."

"We have methods of assisting that should not be considered charity. For example, we understand that ye own this farm free and clear from debt. We can offer thee a stipend, or regular quarterly payments, and grant thee a life estate in thy property. In return thee would sign a contract that the property would belong to the church upon thy death, and we would wish thee a long life."

With emotion, Hancel declared, "I have too many happy memories here. I won't sell it if I can help it. Louie would want me to keep it for his sons. I will hold on to his land," "We are no here to persuade thee, certainly not to coerce thee, or to urge thee to do anything. We merely wish to offer thee a means of keeping thy family together."

When the meeting was concluded the leader suggested that they kneel and pray. As they departed the spokesman reminded her, "Remember, if in the future ye need our help, thou hast only to contact thy minister."

A few weeks later a horse and buggy pulled up in front of the house. A gentleman, in a black suit and a broad brimmed hat, descended and walked up the path. Hancel recognized him immediately as one of the men who had called with the church delegations earlier. She invited him in. After a brief conversation, he asked her to send the children outside to play so they could converse quietly. When they were alone, it was apparent that he was having difficulty stating the purpose of his visit.

"Hancel. May I call thee by thy given name? I have a proposition to make to thee. Nay, that is a poor choice of word. I would like to suggest a possible solution in helping thee in thy widowhood. Please do not take offense at what I am going to say. It may seem strange but hear me out." He paused momentarily.

Hancel, puzzled by his demeanor, merely nodded. The man continued, "Thee is a nice looking woman; clean, soft spoken, and well mannered. My wife is ailing. She is mentally ill. I must treat her like a child. In truth, that is what she is. We have no children. In a sense we have no marriage. Does't thou know what I mean?"

Hancel wasn't sure she knew what he meant, where the conversation was leading. But she answered, "I'm sorry for the two of you. I know the meaning of your words. I'm not sure I know why you are discussing it with me."

"I'm a lonely man. I am still a young man, only forty years old. I miss the companionship of a woman, being with a woman. I'm sure thee knows my meaning. I own a farm over in the next county. I have ample means, and I would be generous if we could make suitable arrangements. I would make it worth thy while."

Hancel, confused and uncomfortable, asked, "What sort of an arrangement are you suggesting?"

"If I could call on thee from time to time; have a few hours alone with thee. When I first saw thee feeling that have lain dormant for years overcome me. I have not only thought of my emotions, I have thought of thy vulnerability. How hard it will be for thee to rear thy children alone. If we could enjoy an evening of intelligent conversation and friendship now and then, form a relationship as a man and a woman, being circumspect and discreet of course. I could help thee financially."

Hancel sat for a moment in silence. Before answering, "But you have a wife."

"Yes, I would do nothing to harm her. I will always take care of her. Thee must understand that. Without a husband thee will also feel needs. I will not rush thee. Take time to make up thy mind." Hancel arose. She walked to the door and opened it. "This conversation is finished. I won't discuss it further. I wish it had never occurred. Good day."

"Hancel, be not hasty in they judgment. Consider letting me drop in from time to time before you dismiss me. Let us come to know each other. I meant thee no disrespect."

"I feel disrespect. I feel shame. I feel sorry that you felt you could approach me with such a proposition. And yes it is the right word. I let you in thinking you were a Godly man.

"Even Godly men have needs."

"The door is open." Preceding him through the door, Hancel called to her children. As they ran by the man tipped his hat, saying, "I hope our conversation will remain strictly between thee and me. If I can ever help thee, don't hesitate to contact me. I will leave my address."

"I will not need the address. I doubt that we will meet again, but if we should I will not embarrass you. Good day."

The man walked down the path, entered his buggy and thumped the reins on the horse's rump as he drove away.

The next time Aunt VI visited, I remember hearing Hancel repeat the above conversation and events of that day as they transpired. As Hancel related the incident, Vi's laughter echoed through the house as she said, "Why that sanctimonious hypocrite! That pious old humbug! I bet he no more has a sick wife than a sick calf! What did he look like? Was he fat and fifty, bald and bulgy?"

"No. He was quite appealing in appearance; strong, muscular, and I think he mentioned forty years as his age."

"Well, too bad you didn't take his address. Tuck his name away in the corner of your mind. You may need it someday."

"Vivian! He has a wife! He will never buy me no peanuts!" — I think that was the first time I heard Hancel use the expression.

Hancel asked a neighbor if he knew anyone who would plow and plant her small acreage on shares. "If you buy the seeds and your boys help me keep the weeds pulled, I will plant a crop for you. If we plant potatoes we can harvest enough for both our needs and still have some to sell for cash. We could also plant some corn and tomatoes."

Hancel bought seed potatoes and Mr. Thorn showed her how to cut them, leaving four eyes on each piece. In cutting the pieces Hancel minimized wasting any of the bulb. She cut chunks containing the required number of eyes, but shaved off a slice here and a sliver there. When the chore was finished she had pots and pans of pieces to cook. She fried a skillet full for supper, and what wasn't used immediately was put to soak in a pail of water and lowered down into the cistern to keep cool. She later told Aunt Vi, "We ate fried potatoes and stewed potatoes, potato salad, and I even used the gruel for making bread. By the time those spuds were gone I didn't care if I ever looked at another one."

Aunt Vi laughed and said, "Hancel, you pinch a penny until it drips. You'll make out alright."

After the land was plowed, harrowed, and laid out in rows, Hancel took sons out into the field to help plant them. She dropped pieces, eyes pointing up and three steps apart, into the rows that Mr. Thorn had plowed. The boys followed behind and covered them with rich black loam.

TAPS COMES OVER THE WIRE

In August 1923 taps came over the telegraph wire: "President Harding, the twenty-ninth president of the United States, is dead."

The black draped train carrying his body passed through towns and hamlets. An entire population turned out en masse as it slowly wound it's way to Marion, Ohio. I remember standing beside the tracks as a black draped train rolled by. It may have been that train. Perhaps it was one carrying dead service men home after the war.

When Aunt Vi came for her regular visit she brought a copy of the Logansport paper from which Hancel read the following account: "President Harding died of a blood clot while in San Francisco, California. He was laid to rest in Marion, Ohio. The wheels of industry stopped, commerce ceased its bustling grind, and the government halted.

From across the continent a host of citizens came to Marion. A light rain fell, misting people as they honored the dead President. Thousands walked by the bier. They lined the streets in front of the house where he grew up, his father's house. Somber skies reflected the spirit of those who knew him.

There was no rank, no favorite, and no class. A line stretched for six blocks. There were high black hats, battered straw hats, and the luster of silk and faded calico. They were all sorrowful, reverent and tearful.

Shortly after noon a local florist wagon drove up and deposited a six-foot, ornately contrived, cross of flaming red flowers. Worked in the center of the cross, with white flowers, were the initials KKK, for the Ku Klux Klan.

An American Legion band delivered selections of Lead Kindly Light, President Harding's favorite hymn. A quartet sang

Nearer My God to Thee. John Pershing, along with twelve Admirals and generals, were honorary pallbearers."

Another news item stated "President Calvin Coolidge is described as a man of silence, talks little but acts positive and vigorously. The nation wishes him success. If he is able to still endless wags of senatorial tongues and give constructive hands and brains a function, he will be a gift of the gods to the nation. There's too much aimless purposeless talk and cheap playing of politics already."

** Information gleaned from an old Logansport paper dated August 10, 1923, and saved through the years by Hancel.

When harvest time arrived, Mr. Thorn plowed the rows and uncovered the potatoes. Hancel and her children gathered them into baskets. The baskets were placed at the end of each row, beside the road. Later, Mr. Thorn arrived by wagon to pick them up. Hancel's share was deposited in the storeroom.

But that wasn't the end of the potato harvest. The next day Hancel took her children out into the field. They diligently searched each row for the small potatoes that Mr. Thorn said weren't worth harvesting. They gleaned enough for several meals. Washed and boiled in their jackets, and fried in bacon drippings, they made nourishing meals for her children.

When the huckster wagon, a traveling grocery store on wheels, made its rounds Hancel bartered potatoes and eggs for staples. The mobile market often left with a chicken, dangling head down, tied to the rear of the wagon. Vegetables from the garden, peas, green beans and tomatoes were canned. Cabbage was shredded into sauerkraut and packed in large crocks. Packages of pasta and fruit arrived periodically from Uncle Tony. Being healthy kids we were always hungry. However, we never went hungry. Hancel saw to that. The fruits of her labor sustained us.

Harvey and Emma visited often. They had a new car. Emma always sat in the back seat, reserving the front for Paula. Her eyesight was becoming worse with each visit.

A CHRISTMAS VISIST FROM THE KKK

Christmas was coming. Hancel wondered how she could make it special for the children. Her merger supply of cash would not allow her to purchase gifts. Packages arriving from Tony and Aunt Vi would be the extent of Xmas.

It was 1924, a time when the KKK in Indiana had grown to number five hundred thousand. An estimated three out of every five white Protestant males belonged. They participated in social as well as political affairs. They sent terror into the hearts of blacks, and lynched them for daring to look at a white woman. They whipped them for merely walking on the same side of the street as a white person. The KKK was anti-Semitic, anti-foreign, and anti-Catholic. During World War One they scorned American born Germans as imagined enemies merely for the dint of their ancestry. I didn't realize it then, but because of that Christmas Eve I learned that not all Klan members were imbued with bigotry, hatred, and arrogance. Many good men joined the Klan for social status, for fellowship under the cross.

Christmas Eve started with Hancel putting a lighted candle in the window. It would guide the Christ child as he wondered the earth blessing all on that holy night. Next she removed a tissue wrapped artificial Christmas tree from a tall cardboard box and placed it on the round oak table. Digging in the bottom of the box she brought out a package of tiny candles, much like those used on a birthday cake. Clustered among the tree branches were tiny metal holders into which the candles were inserted.

As she prepared the tree she told us that Christmas was a time of giving and sharing, and Santa might not be able to bring us many gifts since they must be shared with boys and girls around the world. She made no mention of the fact that there

65

might be slim pickins' at our house since our father was no longer with us.

Lighting the candles, she blew out the lamp and gathered us about her. We watched the flames flicker as the candles sputtered and winked in the darkness. After a few minutes the lamp was re-lit and the candles extinguished, to the cries of "more, more!" But the precious candles had to be preserved for Christmas night.

We hung our stockings in anticipation of Santa's visit. Then telling us to sit in a circle on the floor, Hancel read us the story of the Star of Bethlehem and the baby Jesus. How the three Magi, or wise men, rode their camels to bring gifts to the newborn babe, thus starting the practice of giving gifts at Christmas.

Through the darkness we heard the sound of sleigh bells. As the sound drew near the older boys jumped up and ran to the window. They shouted, "Santa's here!" I ran to the window to see. Peering through the glass I saw a sleigh pulled by two white horses. Seated inside it was a group of white clad, ghostly looking figures. The boys ran from the window as three figures started up the path toward the house.

At the sound of a knock on the door, we all gathered around Hancel. As she opened the door lamplight reflected on three hooded figures, each holding a bag or box. I was afraid to look at the eerie apparitions but curiosity compelled me to do so.

The spokesman told Hancel they had come to bring a small token of Christmas to her and gifts for the children. Opening the door she admitted them. As each handed her a package they wished her a happy holiday. They reminded her of the respect and admiration they held for her deceased husband. Hancel cried. I didn't know if I should cry. I was over my initial fear, reassured by the friendly voices. I thought they were Magi like in the story we had just heard.

As they departed, we ran to the window to watch the prancing horses and to listen to the jingle of the bells as they faded in the distance. The snow glittered like tiny diamonds in the moonlight.

Then we remembered the packages and wondered what surprises they might hold. Hancel inspected each parcel. Wrapped gifts were laid aside to be stuffed in our stockings later. I remember the canned peaches. I can almost taste them now; taste the peaches, smell the candles, feel that first fear. Memories embedded deep in the recesses of my mind, of how hard it was to settle down to sleep, anticipating morning when we could check our stockings.

When Aunt Vi came for New Years Hancel told her, "Tucked in one of the boxes, in a small brown paper bag, were twenty-five one dollar bills. Each Klan member must have contributed a part. I tried to figure out who the men were. The leader, or spokesman, wore a ring on his finger. I took a close look at that ring. If I see it again, I'll recognize it."

A few years later the local restaurant owner approached Hancel to bake pies for his café. For several weeks she went in every afternoon, except Sundays. I heard her tell Aunt Vi, "I'm sure the cafe owner was the spokesman of the Klan group that visited us that Christmas Eve. I saw the ring on his finger. I will never mention it."

As a child, we witnessed cross burnings in the meadow, across the railroad tracks. I'm sure it was burned as a symbol, not in malice. I can never associate those men of our tiny community with the meanness attributed to skinhead radicals of today's Klan. I remember too well the goodness concealed behind masks and hoods on that long Christmas Eve.

THE OLD KITCHEN RANGE

The days were long and hard but Hancel kept busy tending to her children, keeping them warm and putting food on the table. She eked out a living by taking in washings. Her first customers were the local dentist and the café owner. Every week she not only washed but also boiled the linens until they were gleaming white. She soon had more work than she could handle. There was no running water in the house. It was carried from the cistern that sat a few feet from the back door. With no electricity, candles and kerosene lamps were used, as in most homes in those days. My daily chore was to clean the glass lamp chimney in warm soapy water. I also trimmed the wick. Only Hancel was allowed to fill the lamp with oil.

In the summer a fire was built in a brick pit in the back yard. White cloths were boiled in a large metal tub filled with soapy lye water. After the cloths were boiled they were lifted out of the scalding water with a long stout pole, made from a sawed off broom handle. They were then ready to go in the washer. The washer was a wooden tub with a cradle rocker. Pushing the cradle to and fro operated it. We children took turns pushing the rocker. At first it seemed like a game but it quickly transposed to a chore as the novelty wore off. Cloths were fed through a hand-cranked wringer and fell into a tub of cold rinse water. Bluing was added to the rinse water for white articles.

On sunny days the laundry was hung on an outside line to dry. During the winter months the equipment was brought inside and water was heated atop the kitchen range or dipped from the stove reservoir. Cloths were hung on lines strung in the storeroom and draped over wooden racks that folded down when not in use. Flat irons were heated on the stove. A cold iron could be exchanged for a hot one by merely switching the wooden handles. Many nights, after we were tucked in bed, Hancel remained in the kitchen laboring over baskets of laundry.

At the mention of the kitchen range, pleasant memories come flooding back. The oven, designed for baking, was our congregating place on frosty mornings. After crawling out of our warm beds we grabbed our cloths and made a beeline for the kitchen. The first one up got the choice location in front of the open oven door. Shoes were deposited in the oven to be warmed and donned at the last minute before going out into the cold for school, so our toes would be toasty warm.

Returning home from school, as we entered the door, the aroma of freshly baked bread, or cinnamon rolls, tempted our taste buds. Actually they had tantalized us from half a block away. An overhead warming oven kept food warm for late diners. It was also used for resuscitation and resurrection of half dead bunny rabbits, baby chicks, and fledgling birds. Rescued from the cold, and wrapped in a towel, they were deposited in the warming oven. More times than not they were revived and life would go on.

For our morning ablutions, bathing, dish washing, and the earlier mentioned laundry, scalding water was dipped from the reservoir located at the end of the stove. If Hancel had the slightest inkling that we were coming down with a cold she brought out the powdered sulfur. Gathering several pinches in her fingers she slowly sprinkled it over the surface of the stove. Rainbow colored flames flickered and leaped in a staccato dance across the black surface purifying the air. We sucked long droughts deep into our lungs, purging out germs. The healing qualities, doubtful by today's standards, were no less therapeutic than many home remedies of that era, such as asafetida bags worn around our necks to fend of flu, as practiced during the 1918 flu epidemic.

The range was a hungry monster that had to be fed. It was used for cooking as well as heating. Coal was expensive. Railroad tracks lay across the field, behind our house. Open coal cars, with loaded bins, jostled as the train careened over the rails spilling chunks of black coal along the tracks. Often, after a train had passed by my older brothers were sent out to pick up any treasured lumps of this black gold that might have fallen. Firemen, who stoked the engine furnaces, soon learned that Hancel was a widow with five children to keep warm. They often shoveled coal from the hoppers, purposely, for the boys to glean.

Somehow, gathering all the corncobs and wood we could find, added to the coal gathered along the tracks and the fuel that Hancel purchased, the black and nickel monster kept glowing, emitting warmth that enfolding us.

As bedtime approached we spread a blanket on the floor in front of the stove and Hancel read us stories by lamplight. Red eyes blinked through isinglass windows as ours drooped, lulled by the drone of her voice and the warmth from the range. This was during a time before radio or television, even before Rural Electrification.

Mostly I remembered the delicious meals cooked atop the Globe. Dishes fit for a king; slowly stewed chicken with fluffy homemade noodles. In memory I can hear Hancel calling, "Willie, go out and catch that old Rhode Island Red hen. She doesn't lay any more and isn't worth her keep. We might as well have her for dinner." He would chase that chicken around the pen, making a game of the capture, until she would call.

"Now, Willie, you've chased that bird long enough. Stop foolin' around and catch her. I must get it dress before dark." As we gathered around, she chopped off its head, plucked the feathers, dissected the bird, and put it on to boil.

The piece-de-resistance was the homemade noodles, rolled paper thin, dried, cut into long strips, and slowly simmered in a clear rich broth. There must have been magic in that old range, along with Hancel's culinary arts. I know for sure her fried potatoes could never be duplicated in an electric skillet. In an iron skillet, iron on iron, skillet and stove, they produced circles crisp on the outside and tender on the inside. In memory I can almost taste them now; detect the aroma, see the faces, and hear the simple grace being recited, "Bless this food to the good of our body."

JOSEPH'S ACCIDENT

One day Joseph came running home from town and asked for permission to accompany Dr. Zimmer and a group of boys to a Grange Fair. A few hours later Dr. Zimmer's car stopped in front of the house. He lifted Joseph's motionless body from the back seat of the vehicle and carried him up the path toward the house. Hancel saw him coming and opened the door to admit him. Her heart filled with fear at the sight of son lying limp in his arms. As the doctor pushed by her he said, "Hancel, there's been an accident. Your son's is in bad shape. I'm afraid he has a brain concussion. Get him to bed immediately. Send for someone to help you with the other children. Joseph will need all your attention."

After seeing that Joseph was made comfortable, Dr. Zimmer consoled Hancel and promised that her son would be all right. He dashed out the door calling, "I'm going for a nurse. Joe needs constant care."

Willie returned accompanied by Mrs. Thorn. When she asked what had happened, Hancel realized that she didn't know how her son had been injured. She only knew that his life was in jeopardy. For the first time she was overwhelmed by the gravity of the situation. "I've lost my husband. The Lord can't take my son." "Hush! You must be strong. Your son will be all right."

Doctor Zimmer returned shortly, accompanied by a young nurse. After seeing to Joseph, he took Hancel aside to explain the situation. "The boys were having a great time, running races and entering jumping contests. Bags of grains, corn and wheat, were fastened to light poles and strung around the bandstand. Some hung suspended across the road. As the boys raced beneath them, the rope snapped and a bag of grain fell on Joseph. He was stunned for a moment but seemed to be no worse for it. In a short time I missed him. One of the boys said he had gone to the car to lie down. I went immediately to check on him. He had vomited and wanted to sleep. I knew he was in trouble, and I had to get him home."

"Is he going to be alright?"

"Time will tell. I want you to take this tablet, to settle your nerves. Go lie down." You must conserve your strength for what may be ahead."

Hancel sat by the bed for hours. The nurse finally induced her to lie down, but she refused any medication that might make her sleepy. Joseph stirred occasionally. He opened his eyes and drifted back to sleep. By morning he was still in a comma. Dr. Zimmer returned and assured her that Joseph was going to be fine. He finally revived, but the doctor still confined him to the bed. The nurse stayed for three days. When Hancel asked about the charges, Dr. Zimmer said he assumed all blame and there would be no fee. The nurse said she was still in practice training and could not charge anything.

When Hancel told Dr. Zimmer that it sounded like charity to her, he said, "The Lord intended us to be charitable to one another. The Bible says something about Faith, Hope and Charity, and notes that the greatest of these is Charity.

"I thought it was Love."

"Love creates charity. The Lord intended us to be charitable to one another. You must learn to allow people to be charitable, Hancel. It paves their way to heaven.

Despite the fact that she now had two small children Aunt Maudie was not happy merely being a housewife. She opened a hat shop and was soon spending many hours away from home. This did not make Uncle Mike as unhappy as did the fact that she soon took up with a certain drummer. A salesman, who regularly called at her place of business to sell ribbons and flowers, and while peddling his wares, put in a good word for himself. Maudie soon asked for a separation, which in time led to divorce. To make matters worse, and to Uncle Mike's horror, she intended to take the children."

"Take my little Bambinos! Never!"

One day, shortly after the divorce, Uncle Mike showed up at our door. He planned to leave the state and join a sister living in California. With her help he would raise his children. He sought Hancel's assistance in getting ready for the trip. She was not a willing participant in the plot but family loyalty, and concern for the children, induced her to aid and abet him.

All Mike had with him was one change of clothing for the kids and a bottle for the little girl. Hancel went to the dry goods store and bought cotton flannel and made diapers for both children. Uncle Mike bought a ticket to St. Louis. There, he planned to get off the train to purchase another so his route could not be traced. With both kids in diapers, a change of clothing for each, a baby bottle filled with milk, and some sandwiches he caught the mid-night train out of town, and out of our lives forever, except for an occasional letter.

It wasn't long before Aunt Maudie and the law came hunting for him. All Hancel would say was, "I can't tell you anything about him." She could not be swayed from that statement.

Aunt Maudie soon disappeared from town, except for an occasional visit. She came once, sporting a brand new hair-do; bleached blonde and marcelled. Her affair with the drummer faded away, as did her visits.

One day, after Uncle Mike 's departure, as Hancel passed the barbershop the man who had purchased the shop called to her. "Hancel, when your children need a haircut send them in. I will cut their hair free of charge. Louie was a friend of mine. He once did me a special favor. In this way I can repay that favor." She knew that her husband and the man had been friends, but she voiced the oft-repeated words of not wanting any charity by par-a-phrasing the words, — "thanks, but no thanks."

"Don't think of it as charity. I will be honoring my friend's memory by helping his family. There are times when I'm not busy with a customer. I'd as soon be cutting the kids hair as sitting around idle. Instruct them that if I'm busy, to wait until I am free, or return later."

Through the years I felt no aversion about getting a haircut. I didn't realize that we were different from other paying customers. Willie balked every time. He never went until Hancel insisted he do so. He must have known we didn't pay and was chagrined for only saying thanks.

One day Willie came home with his head shaved. He looked like a fuzzed peach. Joseph laughingly admitted that he had talked Willie into the deed by convincing him it would be cooler for the summer. Hancel was furious. She marched Joseph up town and instructed the barber to shave him bald! He sulked for days.

THE ORPHANAGE

Hancel was overworked; tired and worn out. She became ill with pneumonia. When she recovered Dr. Zimmer told her, "No more washing clothes in this cold weather. No carrying water and exposing yourself to the elements. You need a complete rest. If you kill yourself who'll take care of these kids?"

A friend, a do-gooder always prone to offer advise, upon hearing that she was ill came to see how she could help. "Hancel, it seems impossible that you will be able to raise these children by yourself. It might be advisable for you to place them in an orphanage."

"No! I will keep my kids! I will raise them."

"At least consider placing the three older ones in a home. You're wearing yourself out. It won't do you much good to get yourself sick and unable to tend to them. Think about it. At least consider the option for the three big ones."

In a moment of weakness, and physically exhausted and despite her moral fortitude, Hancel allowed herself to be persuaded. Her friend said, "I'll make arrangements for you to check the home. You will see it will probably be the best solution."

I was probably seven years old, maybe eight. I remember that long ride to a big building where children marched in line. They marched to the bathroom, to the dining room, and always seemed to be forming in line. There was a big room filled with long tables with children gathered around it. We ate oatmeal with milk and sugar, and even had a cookie. Joseph looked angry all day. Willie cried. Why was Willie crying? I was having a good time. In one room we played games and sang songs.

After we finished eating Hancel and her friend got into an argument. Hancel rounded us up and said, "We will all leave now. I'm taking my children home and there will be no more talk about them staying at this orphanage!" On the long ride home I listened to the hum of voices in verbal combat until I finally drifted off to sleep.

The next time Aunt Vi came to visit Hancel told her, "When I got in that car and started home, I felt as if a weight had been lifted from me. I knew, as I entered my door with all my kids around me, that no one would persuade me to give up even one of them. I don't know why I let myself be influenced, why I ever considered that orphanage in the first place. We'll all stay together somehow."

"You were only being human. Things had gotten beyond your endurance, but you're a survivor, Hancel. You'll make a good life for your family. I have no doubt about that."

When it was time for Aunt Vi's regular monthly visit, we would all walk to the station and wait for her train to arrive. She always descended the steps with a roll of papers tucked under her arm; funny papers saved from her Sunday editions. Joseph and Willie always raced ahead to be the first to give her a hug, and the first to reach for the roll of comics. After picking up her luggage the boys dashed home ahead of us. The baggage man always gave Louis and me a ride on the freight wagon. By the time we arrived home we would find my brothers stretched out on the floor, flat on their stomachs, with a funny page spread on the floor in front of each one. They were catching up on the antics of the Katzenjammer Kids, Little Orphan Annie and her dog, Sandy, Mutt and Jeff; and there was Barney Goggle. Remember Barney Goggle? —

> Barney Goggle with the goo-goo-googley eyes
> Barney Goggle had a wife three times his size.
> > She sued Barney for divorce.
> > Now he's living with his horse. —
> Barney Google with the Goo-goo- goggle eyes.

Kids today could never have as much fun with all their comic books as we did with those month old funny papers. We read them for days before trading them to friends. We loaned them to kids that had not seen them, and sometimes we hoarded our favorites.

THE OLD ORGAN

One day a wagon pulled up in front of the house. An old gentleman jumped down and walked toward the door. We ran to tell Hancel. When she opened the door, he removed his hat and introduced himself, saying, "Mrs. Benedict, I'm Mr. Gumm. I live out near the river. My wife has this organ that she wants to get rid of but didn't know what to do with it. She thought you might like it for your kids. One of them might have an ear for music and learn to play it."

For a moment Hancel was dumfounded. She looked beyond the man to the wagon and spied the organ, anchored on both sides of the wagon bed, tied down with ropes. A young man sat on the wagon bench. As Hancel hesitated, pondering an answer, I grabbed her around the legs and cried, "Can we have it? I can learn to play an organ. I know I can! Please, can we have it?"

Always willing to oblige her children, Hancel finally said, "Well, let me see where I can put it. Excuse me, while I check around." Returning a moment later she said, "Take it around to the back door. I'll put it in the storeroom where the children play."

Thus we acquired what had once been a magnificent music maker, and an ornate piece of furniture. The ivory keys were yellow with age and streaked with tiny thread like cracks. Two or three pull button knobs were missing. The pedals, once padded with plush, were ragged and fuzzed with worn spots. The top was adorned with two small mirrors surrounded by ornamental railings. Accompanying the organ was a round stool padded with red velvet, which was slightly lumpy. Wobbly, and prone to tip, it still twirled on its pedestal. Twirling was great fun!

Crocks of pickles, peppers, and kraut, barrels and baskets were arranged to leave one wall free to accommodate the organ.

It was placed beside the open stairs that ascended to the attic. The attic roof slopped to meet the eaves and encompassed one large room. I hated the attic and feared it as the dwelling place of the old lady in black, who my brothers teasingly told me lived there. In my desire to play the organ, I stifled my fear.

We took turns pumping the pedals and pounding the keys. We improvised melodies and sang together. I imagined myself a prima donna as I warbled arias and performed to an appreciative audience, my little brother and sister, and neighbor kids. No one emoted more dramatically at their first-nighter than I did in those long ago theatricals. We held mock weddings. Draped in a white curtain, I was the bride and Willie the groom. A little neighbor girl played the wedding march. We held solemn church services. Willie pretended he was Billy Sunday preaching hell fire and brimstone, and I belted out solos of Brighten the Corner Where You Are.

The organ squeaked, creaked, and groaned in abuse. Hancel stood the assaults to her ears, and the loss of tranquility in her home for several weeks. Finally, when cousin Bill arrived for one of his frequent visits she asked him to move the organ into the little barn; where it graced Dolly's old stall. Somehow weddings and church services relegated to the confines of a horse stall did not seem proper. Maybe the acoustics weren't right. The light was too dim and the atmosphere not airy enough. Musical endeavors lost their appeal. Eventually the old organ fell to rack and ruin. Finally, piece-by-piece, it all ended up in the kitchen range. Not, however, before my brothers tore it apart to see what made it play.

During the organ period, when Aunt Vi was on one of her regular visits, Hancel related the tale of the acquisition of the organ and her subsequent headaches saying, "Just because I'm a poor widow woman people think they can dump any old thing off on me. Well! They don't buy me no peanuts and I'm not gonna take it anymore!"

"Now Hancel, admit it. Those kids had a barrel of fun with that organ." Hancel agreed and they had a good laugh together.

After the organ went by the wayside, a little friend and I made a playhouse in their abandoned chicken house. We swept out the old straw, splashed water on the floor and considered it scrubbed. The hen's nest, attached to the walls, became our doll's beds. We retrieved two old milk stools from the barn, and an up side down wooden crate became our table. Finally, tacking up an old scrap of a curtain we proudly surveyed our accomplishments. By the time I was called home I was a filthy mess. Hancel made me strip, gave me a basin of water and a bar of soap and ordered me to wash, at the pump bench, before I could enter the house.

As I sat at the supper table my head began to itch. When we gathered for our evening story I couldn't stop scratching. Noticing me scratching, Hancel asked what was wrong. When she discovered that I had spent the afternoon in the chicken house she instructed me to kneel down in front of her. Upon examining my head she found it crawling with chicken lice. I was exiled to the pump. In the light shining through the open door, she doused my head with kerosene. I screamed, "It burns! Don't get it in my eyes!"

"Serves you right for playing in that chicken house. Don't let me hear of you being in it again." She liberally rubbed oil into my scalp then washed my head in warm soapy water. After repeated dousing, and de-lousing, I was sent to bed. The next day my brothers, for fear they would catch the bugs, shunned me.

In those days kerosene was often used as a home remedy. Taken by the spoonful it was a sure cure for the sore throat. A bit of sugar was added to kill the taste. Luckily, it didn't kill the patient! A double dose was administered for the croup. It was used for chigger bites and insect stings. It was the miracle drug of the day, and cheap at three cents a gallon. Bathed in it at birth, kerosene seemed to be a destiny from which I had no escape.

Hancel led Joseph into the house, gave him a whipping and sent him to bed without his supper. We didn't know why until Joseph related the following story later:

"I found a bag of tobacco and a package of cigarette papers in some of Dad's things. I wondered what it would be like to smoke. I took the tobacco, the papers, and some matches and climbed up on the shed roof. I rolled a cigarette, like I had often seen Dad do it. I lit it and laid back and puffed away. My eyes burned, my head spun, and I got woozy and sick at my stomach. Then I heard Mom calling me. As I stood up to go down I became dizzy and rolled off that slanted roof, and landed right at Mom's at feet, as she rounded the corner of the building."

CHURING BUTTERMILK

Mrs. Worm asked Hancel if I could come and churn butter for her once a week. In payment she would give us all the buttermilk. Hancel, thinking the buttermilk would be nourishing for her children, and for use in baking, said yes. I went once a week to perform the chore. Mrs. Worm always poured the cream into the churn. After the milk had turned to butter, she removed the paddles and scraped them. I washed the churn, the paddles, and all of the bowls.

Mrs. Worm was obese and untidy in appearance. She always reeked of Vicks salve and camphor and complained constantly of an affliction called catarrhal. After preparing the churn she would go to her room and lie down.

One day her two sons lured me away from the churn by offering to show me a moving picture using their Magic Lantern. Dislike of the boys created a moment of apprehension but the desire to see the movie caused me to stifling my fears. I accompanied them upstairs. The projector was set up in a walk in closet. Heat generated by a can of Sterno operated the machine, and a white sheet was draped on the wall as a screen on which the picture would reflect.

When the movie was over one of the boys asked me to pull down my pants so they could look at me. His brother was a willing accomplice. As I tried to crawl out of the closet one boy grabbed me from behind. The other grabbed my feet and tried to yank down my black sateen bloomers. I screamed. A hand clamped over my mouth. I jerked free and kicked as hard as I could. The kick landed squarely in one boy's mouth. As he groaned, I bite the hand held over my mouth and wrenched free. In the struggle I knocked over the flaming can of Sterno. As the boys scrambled to upright the can, I escaped. I dashed down the stairs with both boys in pursuit, calling "Don't you dare tell our mom!"

"I'm going to tell my brothers!"

Hearing the commotion Mrs. Worm called, "Are you boys teasing that girl."

Of course her sons both told her no. I told her the butter was done and I had to hurry right home. Grumbling, she removed the lid and poured the buttermilk into the pail that I always carried with me. I didn't even stay to wash the utensils.

On the next churning day I refused to go. When pressed for a reason I told Hancel, "I can't stand the smell of Vicks salve any more. Make Willie go." I was ashamed to tell the real reason but no amount of persuasion could have induced me to return. Willie complained that it was a girl's job. When Hancel realized that I had no intentions of going back she sent Willie to perform the task.

A few weeks later, the sound of whistles blowing and bells clanging awakened us as a fire engine sped by our house. We dashed outside to see the Worm's barn ablaze. Reddish-orange flames flickered in wild fury as sparks swirled upward in the darkness. Clothed in our sleepwear, we ran down the road for a closer look. Hancel trailed behind shouting to us to stay together and not get separated in the crowd.

Horses whinnied and cows bawled in terror. Men dipped blankets in the watering trough and carried them into the blazing inferno. As a man emerged, leading a horse with a blanket draped over its head, the roof creaked, swayed, and caved in. Men ran helter-skelter abandoning all rescue attempts. They barely escaped with their lives as the sidewalls fell in a smoldering heap around them. In a matter of minutes the huge barn, filled with new mown hay, farm machinery, tools, and animals disintegrated. Nothing remained but ashes, charred wood, twisted metal and skeletal remains of dead animals.

Some thought combustion caused by the new mown hay ignited the blaze. Others surmised that a tramp, seeking shelter, had made his way from the tracks into the barn and fell asleep while smoking. Willie had other ideas. As he churned the butter, that day, the Worm boys tried to lure him into the barn for a smoke. — Thus he was relieved of the task of churning buttermilk.

That was the same year that our well ran dry. To get water to do the washings, Hancel was forced to walk several hundred feet to the last city cistern, used for fire fighting purposes. First, she had to remove the heavy iron cover. This was done by tugging and pulling on an iron ring attached to the lid. She then bailed water, pail by pail, from the cistern. Lugging a full bucket of water in each hand, she trudged home, repeating the process time and again. In order to eliminate the difficult chore of removing the lid each time, I was stationed as a guard by the open well pit. Every time she started home she instructed me, "You sit right where I tell you to. If a child or a dog comes near the hole, you chase it away. Now don't move one inch until I return. Don't go near that hole or you might fall in."

Somehow I realized the danger and obeyed. Looking back, later, we both agreed it could have led to a tragedy, But at that time there seemed to be no other recourse. She did what she had to do. That also became a familiar phrase for her. - "I'll do whatever I have to do." Other phrases were: I'll make out somehow. - Money doesn't grow on trees. We'll get by the best way we can. —We're hanging on. We'll get through this somehow. And of course: "THEY DON'T BUY ME NO PEANUTS!"

HANCEL ASSUMES THE NEWSPAPER AGENCY

One day a man knocked at our door. He introduced himself as James Allan. (Fictitious name) He had been directed to Hancel as a possible agent for the Indianapolis Star. Her job would be to hire boys to deliver the daily paper, or as suggested, perhaps her sons might be able to perform the chore. In discussing the possibilities, Hancel saw it as a means of supporting her family. Joseph and Willie would soon be old enough to help, until then she would assume the task. Besides becoming the agent for the Indianapolis Star, she later acquired the agency for the Indianapolis News, Muncie Star, Marion Chronicle, and the Sunday delivery of the Chicago Herald Examiner. (This early addition arrived in the middle of the week and allowed us a sneak preview of the comics.)

From time to time the gentleman returned to see how Hancel was getting along. Once as he departed, he asked if there was a boarding house in town. "It's getting too late to drive back to Indianapolis. The hotel has closed its doors. I need a room for the night."

Hancel's mind began to click. The spare room was always kept ready for Vi's visits. She could rent it to him. "I don't know of any boarding house but I could rent you a room for the night. I always keep my spare room ready for my sister's visits."

"Are you sure? I wouldn't want to impose on you."

"I would charge you three dollars, if that seems fair to you. If you have not had your dinner, you may take it with us."

"More than fair. Are you sure it isn't too much bother?"

"No. I will fill the pitcher with hot water and the lava bowl is for washing. Joseph will show you the facilities out back."

After dinner he complimented Hancel for the meal, adding that he got tired of restaurant food. He played with the boys until bedtime, and then he tilted his chair back against the house. Hancel was immediately reminded of Louie. As he lit a cigarette she noted the similarity between the two men. After we were tucked in bed, James Allan called to Hancel, "Come sit with me. Rest a bit and enjoy the night noises. It's so pleasant out here."

The next morning Hancel invited him to take breakfast with them; "I'm making griddle cakes for the children. You're welcome to join us, if you like." He stayed and seemed in no great hurry to leave.

As he departed he told Hancel, "I might be caught without a hotel room again. If so, could you put me up again?"

Hancel nodded, "Yes, I'd be happy to."

A couple of weeks later he appeared again. He stayed again. On Aunt Vi's next visit, Hancel casually mentioned James Allan and his nights as a boarder. Aunt Vi wanted to know all about him. "What does he look like? Is he married?"

"No. He's a bachelor. He is handsome and polite; about my age."

"Do I detect an interest there? Are those friendly evenings together apt to lead somewhere?"

Now, Vi, Don't go reading anything into the situation. I can't think of it leading anywhere. I have my children to consider. It's nice to have a little male companionship for a change. In little ways he reminds me of Louie, like the way he tips his chair back against the house; how he rolls his cigarette the same way. The past two years have been lonely without a husband. You know, I am almost glad when I see you coming without your husband, Especially when I see you all lovey-dovey together. Sometimes I could cry. It's been very hard, Vi"

Vi arose, walked over and hugged Hancel. They cried together. James Allan's visit became more regular. Hancel seemed happier than she had been for along time. At night, I could hear their voices, muted in conversation, and drifting back from outside. It seemed right.

A STRANGER AT THE DOOR

One night someone pounding in the back door awakened us. Hancel arose, lit the lamp, and peeped through the curtain. A stranger was standing on the stoop. She called to him and asked what he wanted. The man continued to rattle the door, attempting to open it, as he mumbled something about Gas City. He continued pacing back and forth and trying to open the door. Realized his action was not normal, Hancel encouraged him to go to the house across the street. She rationalized there was a man in that house, whereas she was a woman alone. He finally crossed the street. A light appeared in the window as the door open and the man was admitted.

We were all huddled about Hancel. Biding us to return to our beds, except for Joseph, she instructed him. "Joseph, I am going across the field to Mr. Thorn's house and asks him to go for the marshal. When I go out the door, you lock it behind me and do not open it until I return."

We all begged her not to go, but she said, "That poor man is not rational. He needs help." She slipped silently into the night and we watched Joseph turn the key in the lock. Although she returned quickly, to us it seemed an eternity. She assured us, "Everything will be alright now. Mr. Thorn walked me home on his way to the marshals office."

The next morning, as she walked her paper route, she spied two men lying on a customer's lawn. Recognizing their garments were the same as that worn by the intruder the night before, she laid her paper bag down and walked to the marshal's office. He had taken the one man into custody, and had discovered him to be an escapee from the Soldier's Home in Marion, so he knew the other two were fellow escapees.

After the close of World War One, it was not unusually to witness a disoriented veteran, shell shocked or reliving a war experience, roaming about. One who had strayed away from a family who refused to institutionalize someone they loved.

As spring planting time drew near, Old Mr. Mavis (fictitious name) approached Hancel to inquire if she had hired anyone to till her land. Upon learning that she had not, he said, "Then I'm here to make a deal with you, if we can come to a satisfactory agreement." Hancel invited him in and arrangements were made that he would plant the land on shares. He would also plow a garden spot for her.

A few days later he returned. In fact he stopped often on one pretense or another. Hancel always kept me inside the house with her when he came. One day he stopped and said he wanted to come in and talk about something. Thinking there was something important to discuss, Hancel invited him in and said she would brew a pot of tea. The old gent pulled a paper bag from his pocket and offered it to me, saying, "Look here, Girlie, here's a bag of peppermint candy, all for you. Take it and go out and play."

Hancel immediately intercepted. She took the bag and deposited in the kitchen cupboard as she said, "Julia, you will stay right in this house. The mints will be shared with the other children, later."

As she poured a cup of tea, the old man moved his chair closer to her. In a few moments I heard the noise of a chair scraping across the floor. Hancel arose, removed the cups and saucer from the table, took the tablecloth off and folded it, then replaced the cups on the bare table. With anger in her voice she said, "Mr. Mavis! You will sit on your side of the table and I will sit on mine! I want it understood that anything between is strictly business, no monkey business! Do I make myself clear?"

"Yes, Mum, you do that. No monkey business."

I saw no humor in the incident but Aunt Vi did when Hancel recited the incident to her on her next visit. Laughter pealed forth as she said, "That old goat must not be as old as you think! There's no fool like an old fool who thinks he's a young

Lothario! You might as well resign yourself to more of the same. Some men seem to think a young widow is theirs for the taking." I didn't understand the conversation at that time, but she was right, Hancel received her share of similar advances during the years ahead.

WE MOVED BACK TO THE OTHER HOUSE

Aunt Vi, on one of her regular visits, voiced concern, "Hancel, you're working too hard. You can't continue carrying water and taking in washings with no electricity. You should give your tenant notice and move back to the other house. You wouldn't have as far to walk in delivering paper, and with electricity the washings would be easier, and the children would be closer to school. Rent out this house but retain the acreage."

Hancel said she had been having the same thoughts. A few weeks later we moved from the little farm. Louis remembers that Hancel entrusted him to carry her yellow spatter-paint crock pitcher as his part in the moving process. With electricity and running water in the house Hancel began to save for a new Maytag washer. It was a proud day when she finally saved the last penny to make the purchase.

It wasn't long after the washer was acquired that I returned home from school to a house reeking of antiseptics. Hancel signaled me to be quiet, "Your sister is asleep." Intrigued by the new machine, my little sister had somehow caught her hand in the wringer. Hearing her screams, Hancel turned in time to see the arm coming through the rollers, extending almost to her elbow. She quickly released the pressure on the rollers, reversed the wringer, and ran the arm back through the wringers. She carried her all the way to Dr. Zimmer's office. Luckily, no bones were broken. She awoke as if nothing had happened.

A few days later Joseph caught a wild baby rabbit in a snare. He brought it home for Little Hancel for a pet. She kept it in a shoebox and fed it milk from an eyedropper. Occasionally she let it out to hop about. One day, as Hancel removed garments from the washer to put them through the wringer, she let out a scream as she dropped an object. She immediate realized it was the little rabbit. It had escaped from the box and curled up in a pile of clothing that lay sorted on the floor. It was deposited in the washer along with the soiled clothing. Little Hancel was heart broken.

Hancel began taking house-cleaning jobs. She cleaned Dr. Zimmer's office as payment for his services, or for cash if nothing was owed. Although she worked hard, life seemed easier. When we older children were in school and unable to tend to the two younger ones, they were left with an old neighbor couple. They were happy to have the children's company and, as they said, they could use a little tobacco money. They both dipped snuff and smoked tiny clay pipes, a habit acquired during the years they lived in the hills of Kentucky. The man was an old Civil War veteran. The lady always wore black in memory of her first husband who had died in that war.

Hancel and Julia at other house

One day, as Hancel arrived to pick up the children, the lady brought out a carefully wrapped package and presented it to her, saying, "This is a pair of blue serge trousers that belonged to my first husband. The seat is worn but there's still lot of good material left in the legs. You can make a pair of pants for the little boy."

92

A few days later Hancel was ironing cloths. Louis, playing nearby, began to sing. Hancel, preoccupied with her task, paid no attention to the song. Gradually, as the words penetrated her mind, she stopped ironing to listen to the verse. "Little frog in the pool says knee deep; knee deep. Big frog in the pool says pecker deep; pecker deep."

Hancel asked, "Louis, where did you learn that song?"

Louis innocently answered, "Mr. Wallace taught it to me."

A few days later, upon hearing him utter a few more undesirable expletives, Hancel admonished him. As his vocabulary became spicier she deemed it advisable to find other caretakers. In a few days Mrs. Wallace came to see why she no longer brought the children around. Hancel explained that she managed to go to work when one of the older ones was at home to keep them.

It was a rainy day. To prevent the floors from being tracked with mud, Hancel had spread the old trousers, which she deemed unsuitable for remaking, on the porch as a mat to wipe our feet on. Mrs. Wallace spied the garment and recognized it as her husband's old pants. In dismay she said, "Why, Hancel, I thought you'd use that blue serge material to make a pair of pants for the little boy. If I had known you would use them for a doormat, I would have cut off the buttons and saved them."

Telling her to wait a moment, Hancel entered the house. She returned with a pair of scissor, stooped and snipped off the buttons. She handed them to Mrs. Wallace, saying, "Here's your buttons. Now you can save them!" Entering the door with a bang, she mumbled, "Her and her old blue serge pants! Who needs them? She don't buy me no peanuts!"

VISITING UNCLE TONY'S

In order to instill the traditions of our father's Italian heritage, and perhaps to aid Hancel, Uncle Tony started the custom of inviting my brothers and me to spend the summer months with his family. Sometimes we three older ones went, but often it was just Willie and I. Being devout Catholics, their mores and customs of everyday life were vastly different from ours. Those summers spent in their home shaped our lives immensely.

Cousin Tom loved fast cars and had just bought another new majestic green one. I've forgotten the make but it was sleek and shiny with spoke wheels. A tool chest, resting on a back rack, was filled with tire patching; tire pump, and implements necessary for road emergencies. In those days one entered the car by stepping on a running board. According to Tom, the best feature was the new self-starter; no more hand cranking! In this beauty I made my first trip to Indianapolis, and my first summer away from home.

Uncle Tony was a strict disciplinarian. He disapproved of the frivolity of make-up; rouge, lipstick and nail polish. Cousin Rose, a telephone operator, was up to date and modern in the styles of the twenties. Every morning before leaving for work she applied nail polish. Upon returning home in the evenings she would hastily remove it before Uncle Tony returned from his job on the railroad.

Arriving home early one evening, Uncle Tony sniffed the air and detected the scent of banana oil, used in the nail polish remover. He questioned the origin of the odor. Rose quietly asked me if I had eaten a banana. But she immediately turned in conversation with her sister, allowing me no time to respond. Tony's oldest son, Frank, owned a fruit and vegetable store on Washington Street, a short distance from their house. Each

94

afternoon it was my custom to walk down the alley to the store and select a special treat. That day I had chosen a peach. Rose did not know if I had eaten a banana but offered the following explanation later:

"I used mental reservation in asking if you had eaten a banana and then quickly changing the subject. I did not lie to my father but I instilled in his mind the idea that you might have eaten a banana, and thus the aroma. By doing so I avoided an argument and confrontation. You must never lie but sometimes using a little tact, and mental reservation, prevents friction." For the rest of the summer, no matter what other treat I selected, I always carried home a banana.

The bachelor sons, a barber and the store keeper, arriving home in the evenings would go immediately to the phonograph, crack it up, and put on their favorite record. The barber usually arrived home first. His selections were I Married The Queen of Barcelona and Valencia. When the storekeeper entered the house he would go to the Victrola, remove whatever record was playing, put on his selection, crank up the instrument, and arias by Caruso or music Italiano would swell forth. Disdain permeated his voice as he asked his brother, "Why do you listen to That garbage. The ritual never changed, only the records were switched.

Our house was located a few hundred feet from a crossroad at the edge of town, where a brick road ended and a gravel road began. The last city streetlight illuminated the area, dubbed the corner. It was the neighborhood kids gathering place after the sun went down. Here we played Pussy wants a corner; heist-tail-go sheepie-go; kick the can, hide and seek and any game we might concoct. Often we merely sat along the curb and told ghost stories. When the curfew sounded we all ran for home.

Little Hancel always seemed to be the last one to leave the play area. If we arrived home before she did, Mom would go to the door, and with a certain inflection in her voice, call Sis. She stood holding the door open. As the straggler ducked below her outstretched arm, she would ask, "Why are you ducking? You know you need a whipping for being late." If she thought we needed a whipping we were sent to find a stick to mete out our punishment. She seldom used it but she was a firm believer that sparing the rod spoils the child. The treat of the stick was usually enough.

A friend's uncle owned a hand-cranked phonograph. It had a fluted Morning Glory speaker, and a picture of a black and white dog was painted on the front of the cabinet. Gold letters spelled out the words His Master's Voice. On rainy days, or sometimes at night, we gathered in his parlor. He would put on a celluloid cylinder, cranked up the phonograph and we listened to amusing old records of Uncle Josh and Aunt Nancy Putting Up the Kitchen Stove, and Uncle Josh Swarming Honey Bee. The Baggage Coach Ahead was a sad song. My favorite song was Pretty Redwing.

Few people had a radio and there was no television. We created our own entertainment. We climbed to the rafters of the old log cabin, used for storing hay, and hand over hand; we traversed the length of the building. If we fell we landed in a soft bed of hay, got up, and repeated the process all over again. It was the best of times before the worst of times — the depression.

Headlines announced: FLOYD COLLINS TRAPPED IN CRYSTAL CAVE IN CAVE CITY KENTUCKY. For days Willie went around singing a ballad written to commemorate his death. In lighter moments he sang Does Your Spearmint Lose It's Flavor On the Bedpost over night?

LOUIS AND THE MELONS

Hancel's two fundamental principals were "don't take charity and don't take anything that doesn't belong to you." This she indoctrinated into our minds. To her it was a matter of pride. One day I found a nickel lying on the sidewalk. I picked it up and took it home. When I showed it to her and explained that I had found it, she instructed me, "Take that nickel right back where you found it. Someone has lost it and will come looking for it." Protesting, I obeyed. I laid the nickel on the sidewalk as I had found it.

For two days I passed that coin lying exactly as I had placed it. It seemed a waste for a nickel to lie there doing no one any good. On the third day I picked it up. I went to the store and bought a nickels worth of red-hots and peanuts, mixed. I ate them all by myself. I had never heard of a guilt trip at that time, but I was on one for days. - But I sure enjoyed the peanuts!

One day, Louis went down the street to play with a little friend. They were both about six years old at the time. During the afternoon the boys wondered into a neighbor's muskmelon patch. They picked a melon and returned the friend's house and ate it. When it was time for Louis to go home, he returned to the garden and helped himself to another melon. He took it home and gave it to Hancel. She immediately asked, "Where did you get the melon, Louis?"

"In Mrs. Hayes's garden." Louis answered, innocently.

"Did Mrs. Hayes give it to you?"

"No, Buddy and I picked one and ate it. I went back and got another to bring home for you."

"Well! You can just march yourself back to Mrs. Hayes house and return it! You tell her what you did, and that you are sorry for stealing her melon."

Louis decried the accusation of stealing it, declaring that he merely token it without permission. He refused to do Hancel's bidding. He pleaded and begged, but in the end, Hancel led him, literally by the ear, back to the Hayes house.

She knocked on the door. When Mrs. Hayes appeared, she said, "Louis has something to tell you. He has a confession to make."

Between sobs, laments and tears of remorse, Louis confessed to pilfering the cantaloupe. That is, he admitted to taking it but insisted he had not stolen it. Mrs. Hayes asked if anyone was with him when he picked the melon. Louis stubbornly refused to snitch on his buddy.

Hancel explained that he had eaten one melon, and asked how much he owed for it. Mrs. Hayes, knowing that Louis was being taught a lesson, replied, "I think a fair price for Louis to pay for the melon he took without my permission would be a dime. What do you think, Hancel? My flower garden needs weeding. Louis can pull the weeds in payment."

Louis worked diligently weeding the flowerbed. When he reported to Mrs. Hayes that the chore was finished. She told him, "You've done a fine job, Louis. I think I owe you another melon. We have more than we can use. Let's go find the biggest, sweetest one in the whole patch. Now promise me that you'll never take anything again without permission."

Louis proudly arrived home with the melon he had earned. Hancel was a bit skeptical. She quizzed him to make sure he had not, again, helped himself to another without permission.

James Alan's visits became less frequent. His letters arrived posted from various cities. When he did appear they had little time to themselves. Children were always present. The bond between them was apparent to me, as young as I was; a shy touch, quick embrace, or a kiss followed by a hasty breaking apart as a child entered the room. I was unconcerned about their relationship. But now, thinking back and remembering snatches of conversation between Hancel and Aunt Vivian I know the two had their moments of amour.

Hancel had a new gentleman friend, a bachelor farmer named Evan. He owned one of the first automobiles in town when they could be numbered on my fingers. Our back yard peach tree produced the sweetest peaches ever tasted. One day Hancel made us a peach cobbler. She also made a pie for Evan. She took special pains fluting the edges and brushing the top with cream to make the crust crisp and brown. As she removed the pie from the oven it somehow spilled and tipped up side down on the kitchen floor. I made the mistake of laughing. This angered Hancel. She said, "Now, young lady, for that little snicker you get busy and clean up this mess." As time passed, Hancel asked us if we would like for Evan to become our father. Joseph or Willie perhaps both, answered no. The romance ended, as always, in deference for her children.

VALENTINE BOX OF CANDY

During Evan's courtship, as Valentines Day neared, he brought her a beautiful red, heart shaped, box of candy. A red velvet bow adorned the satin lid. It was the most beautiful thing I had ever seen. Aware that it was an expensive gift, Hancel put it in the cupboard out of sight. She also knew that it had been purchased at the local drug store. The next day she put the box in a paper bag and instructed me to return it to the store and request a refund. When I voiced my disappointment she promised to make us a batch of fudge adding that the refund money could be used for more important things. - Probably food.

Ours was a small town. Very few happenings went unnoticed and all soon became common knowledge to the entire community. The druggist, remembering who had purchased the candy, asked me if Evan was sparking my mom. He "allowed" he could give me a refund if he discounted the original price since if the item didn't resell before Valentines Day, he would lose money. Even so, the amount of the refund sounded like a lot of money to me. I accepted it and hurried home. I gave the money to Hancel and reported the druggist's conversation.

"He'll sell the candy again, make his profit and still come out ahead. So! He knows who gave me the candy, does he? A person can't do anything in this town without it becoming common knowledge! It doesn't matter. The refund money will come in handy. Don't tell Evan that I returned his gift." The next day she made us a batch of fudge.

It seemed a never-ending job just keeping food on the table. Joseph was a big help. In the summer he fished. He not only brought home fish. He caught turtle, which was fried or made into soup. Having somehow acquired a gun, he hunted for rabbit in season. He also trapped. If he caught, or shot, more rabbits than we could eat, he took them to the grocery store and sold them. The only requirement was that the two hind feet must be left on the animal so as to differentiate a rabbit from a cat.

Once he caught a possum. A fellow hunter told him roasted possum made a good meal, especially with yams added around the roast. That idea did not appeal to Hancel. She absolutely refused to cook it! Joseph baked it, adding sweet potatoes at just the right moment. It smelled sweet and sickening, and tempted no one except Joseph. He ate it with gusto! Hancel made him wash all the pots and pans, and admonished him, "Don't ever bring another one of those repulsive animals in this house again!"

Each spring, sassafras roots were gathered and brewed into tea. Actually, it was administered as a spring tonic. We gathered tender young dandelion greens for salad, and to be cooked like spinach. When berries season rolled around, we picked wild strawberries and raspberries.

At hog butchering time a farmer friend always brought Hancel a pig liver. He first had to convince her that she was doing him a favor by accepting it. He always butchered two pigs but could only use one liver. Due to the mild weather, and lack of refrigeration, there was no way to preserve the other. It would go to waste if she did not take it. Scalded, rolled in flour and fried with onions, it was nutritious, filling, and good. I have since heard it said that pig liver isn't fit to eat, only beef liver. We ate it and relished it, as we ate whatever was put before us.

Joseph always took good care of his gun. He cleaned it and made sure no shells remained in the chambers before storing it away. But a gun in the house worried Hancel, and we had standing orders to never touch the gun. But orders were sometimes disobeyed, as Louis remembers.

"Kids didn't have many toys in those days. I would get Joe's gun out to play cowboys and Indian with it. I 'd chase Sis around, whooping and hollering. Sometimes I 'd be a cowboy, other times an Indian. I'd always put the gun back in it's proper place before Mom got home, and of course, Joe never knew. He cautioned us about the gun as much as Mom, especially after his friend Sonny shot himself." The following is Joe's tale of Sonny's mishap with a gun:

"Ole Sonny was always a bubble short on brains, anyhow. One day as I was visiting he got out two of his old man's guns. I knew he shouldn't be messing around with those guns, so I left. Sonny was in his upstairs bedroom. I had just walked down the stairs and out the door when I heard a shot and Sonny's scream. Then I heard his mother scream. I dashed back up the stairs there was Sonny laying on the floor with his leg all covered with blood. For reasons know only to Sonny, he had tried to ram the barrel of one gun down into the barrel of the other gun. One gun went off and shot him in the leg. His mother asked me to run and get Dr. Zimmer. Luckily the damage could have been worse, but Sonny was pretty sore for a couple of weeks."

MAKING HOMEBREW

It was time for our annual visit to Uncle Tony's. The family now lived on a farm at the outskirts of Indianapolis. He farmed the land with a team of horses and the aid of his three sons. When we visited we also helped perform chores. The day before market day, green beans and peas were picked and packed; tomatoes and cucumbers were buffed and attractively layered in baskets; radish and onions were cleaned and tied ten to a bunch. Before bunching, the outer layer of the onionskin had to be peeled off. I hated the job. The onions made by eyes burn. If I complained cousin Angie would say, "We will recite the Hail Mary to make the task easier and over more quickly. You will forget that your eyes burn." My eyes didn't burn any less, nor was the chore any easier, but perhaps it helped her in deciding her vocation. She became a teaching nun a few years later.

At Sunday mass, the two younger cousins served as alter boys; Angie sang in the choir, and I got stars in my crown for fanning Sister Rose as she played the organ. Bachelor sons arrived home for Sunday dinners. After a big meal they stretched out on the sofa for an afternoon nap until time to listen to a ballgame on the radio. Any loose coins that fell from their pockets were treasures for me to find and keep. I'm sure that some was intentionally lost.

Sunday dinners was usually a banquet consisting of fresh homegrown vegetables, salad, and deserts, and often chicken. The first time the platter was passed to me I almost dumped the contents in my lap when I spied the chicken head resting on the platter. Glazed eyes seemed to stare from the sockets. I asked, "Do you eat the head of the chicken? I didn't know anyone ever ate the chicken head!"

Cousin Mike quipped, "It's Pa's favorite piece. He likes to pick its brain." I stared in horror as Uncle Tony ate the brain, picked the eyes out, and finally ate the whole chicken head.

Since I was only a girl and often got the attention that he ordinarily received, cousin Mike merely tolerated me. In a rare moment when he did acknowledge my existence he pulled a hair from one of the horse's tail and placed it in the watering trough. As I watched him swish it around in the water he said, "If you check this tank every day you'll find this horse hair will turn into a snake. Sometimes it takes a couple of days."

I checked the tank daily. In a few days there was a snake swimming around in the water. I thought it was magic! The magic was in waiting until he found a snake; magic in the imagination.

Uncle Tony was a large man with a droopy mustache and a huge appetite. He could consume a pitcher of beer, pausing only once, before the last drop was swigged down. Even though it was during Prohibition, Aunt Mary mixed a batch of homebrew weekly. On washdays, between tubs of suds for the laundry, she bottled another suds, foamy home brew that had been set to work and ferment the previous week. Bottles had to be washed and thoroughly rinsed. Between washing cloths, mixing and bottling the illegal brew, it was an all day chore.

Aunt Mary siphoned the amber liquid through a rubber hose by sucking it through the tube. When the beer flowed she pinched the hose together shutting off the liquid until the hose was inserted into a bottle. With a release of her finger the bottle began to fill. This process continued until the last bottle was filled and ready to be capped. Bottles were stored in a dark corner of the cellar until the next washday. Crocks and bottles were washed again, and she stirred together sugar, brown, sweet smelling malt, yeast and other mysterious ingredients. She covered the crock with a clean white cloth and it was left to bubble and brew. A pitcher of the rich amber colored liquor always sat on the table in front of Uncle Tony at suppertime.

One of my daily chores was to listen for Uncle Tony to whistle. Wherever he was plowing or planting, at exactly eleven o'clock every day, his whistle signaled me to bring him a ration of the liquid sustenance. He had already instructed me on the proper way to pour the contents from the bottle into the pitcher, tipping the bottle at just the right angle so as not to rile up the dregs in the bottom.

When I arrived at the field, Uncle Tony stopped the horses, removed his battered straw hat, and mopped his brow with a big blue bandanna handkerchief. Then tipping the bottle, he consumed half of its contents before stopping. It took two bottles to fill that pitcher. If I had poured the elixir just right, without roiling the settlings, he wiped the foam from his mustache, smiled, and patted me on the head, and said, "Tu sei una piccola Santa!" If I accidentally messed up the malt and the yeast he would frown and say, "Tu sei una diavolette." I thought the words were cuss words because of the frown and his demeanor. I didn't know the meaning of the words but I understood the facial expression.

When I returned to the house if I asked Aunt Mary and Angie the meaning of the words in the first phrase, they would smile and pat me on the head. When I asked the meaning of the second phrase they would shake their heads, gasp, and cover their mouth with their hands. It was many years later that I finally learned the first phrase was interpreted, as "you are a little saint." The second was "You are a little devil."

This lesson in making homebrew was vastly different from the training I received from the good ladies of our church, stanch members f the WCTU; Women's Christian Temperance Union. On one Sunday every month, we children were marched up to the stage and recited little ditties they taught us. Like:

> Cigars are bad.
> Cigarettes are worse.
> I'll never chew tobacco,

Safety first.

Along with the little ditties we made solemn vows never to let whisky or Demon rum pass our lips. We signed a pledge promising never to drink distilled, fermented or malt.liquors; included wine, beer and cider. We were also to discourage the sale of the same.

One evening the WCTU ladies were to hold a special session. They hoped to attract the older, the more mature crowd, young men who had been exposed to the dangers of the gin mills. They would offer salvation to a hard drinker or two. Although Willard and Wilbur Worm could not be classified as mature, they came prepared. Word had been passed to their cohorts not to miss the meeting as they intended to make it a corker.

They filled an empty whiskey bottle with tea, stashed a bag of tobacco in their pocket, with the drawstring hanging out, and added a pack of cigarette papers. They waited for the call for all sinners, drinkers, and smokers to free themselves from the grasp of the Devil, to come to the altar and pray with the good ladies for salvation.

At the proper moment, with all eyes riveted upon them, Willard and Wilbur marched up to the altar. Lamenting their wicked ways, one removed the tea filled whiskey bottle from his hip pocket and plunked it down on the altar. The other produced the tobacco and cigarette papers, held them high for all to see, and laid them beside the supposed whiskey. Crying and sobbing, in mock solemnity, they both vowed never to puff another wicked weed or swallow one more drop of booze. The ladies, convinced they had saved two souls from damnation, gathered around the boys offering solace and prayers of thanks for the misguided boys having seen the light.

Joseph, thinking it was funny, reported the incident to Hancel the next morning. But he was admonished, "I'd better never catch you pulling a stunt like that!" Remembering how I helped bottle homebrew and toted it to the field to Uncle Tony, I thought the good ladies would surely have a hay day if they knew of my degradation!

Much of our social activities centered on the church. It was our social gathering place as well as our place of worship. We held Easter Sunrise services; Christmas programs, parties, caroling, and chorus sessions. Every summer we held a picnic at a park called the Wa-wa-na-see Glens, located on the banks of the Mississinewa River. The site had once been an Indian village before their long march on the Trail of Tears. An old Indian, named Nottingham, was still retained as a caretaker.

Penny suppers were held as entertainment as well as for a money making project. Everyone carried in a covered dish of his or her favorite food. It was sold for pennies or nickels a helping. Funds raised by these events were used for hayrides, picnics and other social events, as well as to send representatives to Quaker Haven, a youth summer camp on Lake Wawasee. Although church services were solemn and inspiring, and we venerated the house of the Lord, humor was not missed if it unfolded before our eyes.

One old couple habitually dozed off during services. First her head would start to bob, and then, as it sagged to her bosom, tiny snorts become audible. They grew and expanded into long resonant snores that reverberated from the deacon's bench to the hallelujah corner. Finally, her husband's poke would awaken her. Startled to attention she would shout "Amen!" Soon the husband would doze off, fall asleep, and the whole process was repeated. The Amen chorus continued until church was dismissed. Often, both had to be awakened and started on their journey home. As teen-agers, we laid odds, usually a stick of gum, on which one would be the first to yell "Amen."

We witnessed the true drama of that old time religion when the Pentecostals held a revival, or summer tent meeting, in the park. The tempo of those services, in contrast to our sedate church services, provided a weeks entertainment. When filled with the Holy spirit an emotional worshiper might not only shout Amen, he, or she, could invoke actions more in keeping with a three ring circus. To those less concerned with their souls it could be downright entertaining. To the thump of the piano, and strumming guitars, their hymns burst forth to the tunes of When You Wore a Tulip and I Wore a Big Red Rose, and She Wore A Yellow Ribbon. At one summer session Wilbur and Willard repeated their charade of being saved. The second performance out did the first since we all knew it was a hoax.

Winter revivals were held in the Town Hall, which was heated by a huge coal consuming baseburner with isinglass windows. One night an ardent worshiper, speaking in tongues and filled with enthusiastic fervor, tried to crawl into the stove. Rational members subdued the zealot as he screamed. "Let me go, Brethren! Let me go! The Lord will protect me. He saved Shadrach, Meshach, and Abednego from the fiery furnace. He will save me too."

It was difficult for me, after a summer at Uncle Tony's, praying the Our Father, the rosary and repeating the Hail Mary, to listen to the condemnation of Catholics by alleged ex-nuns who preached at these tent meetings. In disbelief, I heard Catholics referred to as godless heretics who worshiped the Pope. In their ignorance they alluded to the Pope as the Disciple of Satan who ordered priests to consign all illegitimate babies to a flaming incinerator. Political aspirants swore that someone called the Happy Warrior was indeed a member of Satan's army, and if elected would install the Pope in the White House. None of this was consistent, or reflective, of the pious people (despite brewing beer) whom I visited during the summer months, and with whom I attended the quiet Sunday masses. It left me muddled and confused. If I approached Hancel seeking answers for questions that puzzled me, she said I would have plenty of time to find my own answers when I grew up.

Another form of entertainment was shrivarees, or bellings, held for newly married couples. A string of tin cans and old shoes was tied to the bumper of their car. After the newly weds retired for the night, well-wishers arrived to beat on pots and pans, blow whistles, and ring cow bells, thus the term "belling the bride." Bedlam would continue until the gang was admitted, and treats were passed out. Often, older boys managed to sneak into the bedroom and slip a snake between the sheets, or sprinkle bedding linens with itching powder. Any torment was fair to plague the pair. It was accepted in the spirit of fun in which it was participated.

Halloween pranks practiced in those days didn't compared to those of today. We didn't trick or treat. We attended parties in outlandish attire; or disguised and masked we went from door to door to let friends guess who we were. We made tic-tack-toes out of empty wooden spools by notching the edges. The spools were wrapped with string and placed against the window. As the string was pulled the spool spun against the glass and created an eerie sound frightening those inside the house. We tossed corn on porches and pelted it against windows. The next morning the corn was swept up and scattered to the chickens. Those tricks were nothing compared to those perpetrated by the older boys, whose favorite trick was tipping toilets.

One year, an old bachelor, noted for his miserly manners and stingy ways, found his privy turned over the day before Halloween. Seeing the Worm boys pass by his house he called to them to lend a hand in up-righting the outhouse. They toiled hard resetting the privy in its proper place. When the task was finished the old man said, "Thank you, boys. I'll see you up town some day and buy you a pack of gum." The boys, anticipating something a bit more rewarding than a pack of gum, returned the next night and tipped the toilet again. Not content with merely tipping it, they generously smeared contents from the pit on his doorknobs and porch steps.

The next day the old man spied the Worm boys again. Remembering how kindly they had helped him on the previous day, he asked if they had any idea who might have pulled such a dastardly deed on a poor man a second time. They answered, "It was probably those Dago boys down the street."

Seeing Hancel passing by later the old man waylaid her and recited the episode of the tipped toilet, and following events. He didn't directly accuse her sons of the deed, but implied it. Hancel convinced him otherwise saying, "My boys wouldn't do such a trick, and they didn't leave the house last night."

And then there was Alvin. The name Alvin alone was derisive enough, but coupled with his last name, it made him the butt of many jokes. Alvin had a pet pig named Pansy. He loved that pig better than any man loved his best beagle hound. He bathed it, pampered it, and fed it tasty tid-bits. The pig was so fat it waddled. Alvin led Pansy, on a leash, for walks about town. Actually, the pig drug Alvin. It invaded the neighbor's gardens, swilled down succulent green cabbage, chomped on tender young stalks of corn, gobbled up peas from the pea patches, tipped trash barrels and annoyed the entire population of the town.

Pansy was housed in a shed with a flat top roof. One year, the day before Halloween, Alvin went out to feed the pig. The pig was gone. Hearing noises on the rooftop, Alvin ran out and looked up. There, pacing back and forth on the shed roof was Pansy. Alvin yelled for his mother. He jumped up and down and performed one histrionic after another. How would he ever get poor Pansy off the roof?

A neighbor, hearing the commotion, took pity on the boy and suggested that he run to the marshal's office and direct him to blow the whistle and call the volunteer firemen to the rescue. By the time the siren stopped blowing, and the fire engine arrived, half the town had turned out to watch the rescue. To hear how Pansy ascended to the shed roof, to wonder and question. The big question was how did the pig get on top of the roof? Who put it there? That remained a mystery, but in some minds there was little doubt. Most bets were on the Worm boys!

BARNSTORMING PILOTS

It was again time for my yearly visit to Uncle Tony's. When I arrived at the Indianapolis Interurban Terminal it was packed with impatient people shoving and calling for unseen passengers they were to meet. Alone, I was frightened by the enormity of the station and the unfamiliar faces surrounding me. After what seemed an eternity, I spied Cousin Frank coming toward me.

Collecting my baggage, Frank led me through a vast area of loading docks, parked trucks and a few wagons to arrive at his wood-paneled truck. He moved it a few feet before another vehicle blocked his way. In frustration, Frank honked his horn. When the other truck didn't move, he insistently gave several more beeps on the horn. The other driver, equally agitated, angrily shouted a series of profanities and called, "You dam Dago!" Frank retaliated, "Who you callin' a Dago? You dumb Hunky! I oughta' get out and poke you right in the nose!" I thought they would come to blows. But the other driver belligerently shoved his truck into gear and drove away.

I told Frank how other kids, when angry at us, called us Dago. He said, "Don't let it bother you. It's only an expression that was attached to Italian people before they left the old country. Not being sure of the day their ship was to leave for America, they would walk down to the wharf and ask, 'Is it the day to go?' This annoyed the dock officials. When they spied them coming they would say, 'Here come those dam day-goers again.' That led to the derogatory title being attached to all Italians. Every race is ridiculed by one nickname or another."

"My mother says it's ethnic, and we shouldn't be ashamed of it."

"Your mother's right. Just be proud of your heritage. Many great people were Dagos."

Every morning I walked across the field to a neighbor's house, an elderly Dutch couple named Gottlipe. I washed their dishes, including the breakfast dishes and the cream separator bowls. For this chore I earned ten cents per day. As I washed the dishes, Mrs. Gottlipe fed her chickens and sometimes picked vegetables. Having been instructed, "Never go into the parlor" the room became a place of intrigue and mystery to me. One day, I heard a faint noise emanating from the room, and tiny feet were visible below a crack at the bottom of the door. When Mrs. Gottlipe returned, I told her, "Mrs. Gottlipe, there's a fairy in your parlor."

"Och! Girl! Why do you think there is a fairy in my parlor?"

"Because I saw its feet under the door."

"Now there is no fairy in there. Come I will show you."

As we entered the room a mouse dashed across the floor. Mrs. Gottlieb screamed and climbed upon a chair as she yelled, "Quick, get the broom. Get the broom." Needless to say, by the time I returned with the weapon, the mouse had disappeared. It soon became apparent that she had reported the episode to her husband. He teased me about the fairy for days.

Often as I started back across the field, Mr. Gottlieb would call to me and ask if I wanted to earn another coin. Leading me to the corncrib, he showed me how to insert an ear of corn into a corn sheller, turn the crank and grind the corn off the cob. After I finished shelling the corn, he often led me to see his baby goslings, or little chicks. Perhaps he merely pointed out how his crops were growing. Not having a father, I enjoyed these moments. He was like a kindly old grandfather. He often asked if I would like to come live with them. Later I learned that this childless pair told my aunt that they would take me as their daughter if the widow woman would permit it. She assured them that Hancel would not part with a single one of her children.

The Dempsey - Tunney fight was to be broadcast on the radio. Bachelor sons came home to hear it. Each voiced an opinion that their favorite would be the winner. Uncle Tony had his own idea, saying, "Tunney will win because he is Catholic." His sons scoffed at him, but could not convince him that Catholicism had nothing to do with pugilism. They didn't have to. Tunney won, hands down.

The younger boys, Mike and Jim, were avid baseball fans. Every Sunday afternoon they were off attending a game, or playing in one. Their hero was Babe Ruth, the Babe, also known as the Slugger. But Mike soon acquired a new hero to worship, Lucky Lindy, Charles A. Lindbergh. The Kid had flown across the Atlantic, solo, in a plane called the Spirit of St. Louis. Mike lauded his hero daily. Uncle Tony didn't have much faith in airplanes saying, "The flying machine will be a passing fad; it's doomed. Man was not meant to soar in the air like a bird or God would have created him with wings. But after World War One, and Lucky Lindy's oceanic flight, the flying machine was here to stay.

It soon became apparent that Lucky Lindy wasn't the only one who could fly a plane. Airplanes began appearing in cow pastures all over the country. Barnstorming pilots offered rides for a penny a pound. Merchants hired these daredevils for advertising purposes. One day Willie came home with exciting news. "Lucky Lindy's going to fly over town tomorrow. He'll drop leaflets from his plane. Anyone finding one will get a prize from the store with its name on the paper." It wasn't Lindbergh, but in those days all pilots were elevated to a hero's status, man of the hour right up there with Charles A., and every boys hero.

The town buzzed with excitement. Any boy worth his salt planned to be on hand to capture one of the coveted vouchers. I wanted to go with Willie but he quickly informed me that no sister was tagging after him that day. Even though the event wasn't scheduled until one o'clock, Willie headed to town bright and early that morning. Boys banded together savoring every minute. Their eyes scanned the sky anticipating the arrival of the plane. By the time Hancel arrived, accompanied by Louis, Sis, and myself, half the town had assembled. We selected a spot at the end of the first bridge and waited. The droning hum of a motor and a tiny black speck on the horizon announced that the plane was approaching. Within minutes, it soared overhead, swooping and diving dangerously low to the ground and the crowd amassed below.

Tiny white leaflets were released into the air and fluttered to earth as murmurs and screams issued from the crowd. Everyone scrambled in confusing as they tried to catch one of the papers fluttering like confetti above them. Chits landed in treetops and drifted into clustered throngs of humanity mingled in various spots about town. Shouts of jubilation announced the capture of a coveted prize.

My eyes riveted upward as I watched the plane. Finally I became aware of a white object fluttering a few feet away. I scampered to retrieve it. Clutching it securely, I brought it to Hancel. She opened the folded sheet of paper and read: "Free to the bearer, one gallon can of Blue Bird apricot halves. Courtesy of Miller's grocery."

Willie was also lucky. His slip entitled him to a free pair of shoes from Branford's shoe shop. It was debatable which he savored most, the treasure hunt, the prize he claimed, or the memorable exploits of the heroic pilots.

As Lindy was gaining fame and reputation, another dude, high in the sky, was attracting attention and making a name for himself as an exhibitionist. His fete was not as daring, nor his fame as enduring, but Shipwreck Kelly entertained the nation perched atop a flagpole for a record breaking forty-nine days. He sat countless dreary hours through sun, rain, and dark of night performing an accomplishment that faded from the annals of time as a bit of trivia. A feat of daring-do that was no less noteworthy than gobbling up goldfish or crowding into telephone booths, exploits perpetrated by a later generation of attention seekers.

HANCEL BOBS HER HAIR

When planting time rolled around again Grandpa Mavis suggested popcorn as the crop. The ritual of plowing the land, disking, sowing seeds and watching them grow began all over again. When the shares were divided Hancel puzzled how to dispose of the popcorn, at a profit.

First, the corn had to be shelled. Every night the boys carried in a bushel, or two, from the storage shed. After seating us on the floor, Indian fashion, Hancel gave each of us a pie pan and read stories to us as we shelled the corn. Because of the sharp tipped kernels the corn was called squirrel tooth popcorn. After an evening of shelling kernels off the cobs our fingers were frayed and fuzzy. The skin was often rubbed raw.

The corn was packaged in one-pound bags and sold or bartered at the grocery store, sold to neighbors, and traded when the huckster man came around. It was peddled to anyone who would buy it. When a medicine show arrived in town it wasn't hard for Hancel, an attractive young widow tearfully relating that she had five children to raise, to be granted permission to sell popcorn during intermission.

The main attraction was Indian Joe. He claimed to have learned the secrets of herbs and the curative powers of potions from an ancestor, the shaman of his tribe. His accomplice was a beautiful maiden dressed in white doeskin. Fringe on her skirt bottom flounced and flapped with each step she took.

The show was held two nights in order to catch those who might have missed it the first time. For days preceding the show, posters were tacked up around town advertising the event, and every kid who saw one bally-hooed the event. On the night the show opened Hancel took down her big iron skillet and popped skillet, after skillets full, of corn on the kitchen range. It was covered with melt oleo, and scooped into brown paper bags —

obtained by bartering popcorn at the grocery store. The bags were placed in two large wooden baskets, each holding twelve bags. Joseph and Willie each carried a basket to the town hall to be sold to the assembled crowd. I tagged along to watch the show.

The performance consisted of Indian Joe performing rope tricks, reciting jokes, and dancing Indian dances with the buckskin maiden. At intermission, and at the closing, medicine was hawked. With oratorical zeal, the barker listed the curative powers of the elixir. It was a sure cure for all aches and pains. It healed lumbago, gout and other equally annoying ailments, real or imagined. It could regulate the bowels, rejuvenate the weary, and strength the muscles. It's restorative powers calmed the nerves, purified the blood, and it was even good for St.Vitus Dance. It contained no alcohol, opium or drugs, and was probably sassafras colored water sweetened with syrup, herbs, and hokum. It was a patented placebo with powers, so claimed, to prolong life. The scantily clad maiden sashayed through the crowd boosting sales by merely flashing her winsome smile.

Joseph and Willie sold popcorn during intermission and dashed home for refills to sell to people as they exited the hall. Sales were so successful we began selling it at civic affairs, parades, and band concerts. Wherever a crowd gathered we were there selling popcorn.

Hancel's hair was a beautiful chestnut brown that reflected luxuriant highlights. Tendrils curled about her forehead and ears, and tresses hung to her waist. She usually twisted it into a bun at the nape of her neck and pinned it with brown celluloid hairpins. Sometimes she coiled it in braids around her head.

A barrel always sat under the downspout, at the corner of the house, to catch the soft rainwater. Basins of water were bailed from the barrel and heated atop the kitchen range for washing her hair. She used Packer's Tar Soap as shampoo. To remove the lather it was rinsed, twice, in cold water. The tar soap left her hair smelling fresh with a scent of the piney woods. As she prepared to retire for the night, she gathered her hair to one side and plaited it into one long braid. Every morning the kinks left by the tight braids were brushed out. With each stroke of the brush the hair snapped and cracked in flashes of electricity. I loved to lie sleepily in bed and watch this morning ritual.

While performing her daily chores she often wore a dust cap. The bun was tucked snugly under the elastic hem. In cold weather she donned an old red knit bonnet that buttoned beneath her chin. She wore it constantly going in and out of the house to hang up cloths, to take them down, and to run a million and one errands. Sometimes in the rush to get a meal on the table she occasionally forgot to remove the hat before sitting down to eat. This allowed us to chide her, as she often did us, "Take off your hat before sitting down to the table."

For some reason Willie detested that old red bonnet. One morning, as he put on his cap and coat before leaving for school, he spied it hanging on a peg beside his coat. He stuffed it in his pocket and walked out the door. Hancel, ever alert to the antics of her offsprings, didn't miss much. She saw him pocket the hat as he called good-bye. Wondering what he was up to, she ran to the window to watch. When he neared the corner he tossed the bonnet under a clump of bushes. Hancel retrieved it. It adorned her head as she greeted him when he arrived home from school that evening. It became a regular tug of war preserving that old bonnet from her number two son. He would hide it and she would fine it. What ever became of it remains a mystery.

Aunt Vi arrived sporting a brand new bob. With misty eyes, Hancel said it looked appalling. Aunt Vi said she would never go back to the trouble of caring for long hair. She tried to convince Hancel that she should have her hair bobbed. She refused to conform to the fashion.

She would not cut off what she considered her best feature, her long silky brown hair. As time passed, the style caught on. Women were no longer looked upon as hussies for bobbing their hair. Hancel began to realize the time and effort consumed in caring for long hair. Finally, succumbing to the mode of the day, she had her hair bobbed.

I'll never forget the look on Willie's face when he first saw her hair had been cut. He dashed out the door, with a bang. When he didn't come in for supper, I was sent to find him. I found him in the coal shed. He had been crying and refused to come to dinner. For days, he was silent and downcast. He ignored Hancel and refused to talk to her. In time he reconciled and accepted the situation.

The bob, as much as anything, symbolized the Jazz Age, the Roaring Twenties, the Vamp and the Flapper. An era characterized as "a time of bootleg gin and back seat sin." The Flapper acquired her title from the flapping sound made by her four buckle goulashes, which were never fastened. Clad in short skirts, rolled silk stockings, and dangling strings of jet-black beads, with tassels on the ends, she tiptoed through the tulips, tippled bootleg booze and wiggled as she walked. She danced the Charleston, shimmied the Black Bottom and coined the phrases "Oh You Kid! and "Twenty-three skid-do!" She was the cat's meow! As cute as a bugs ear! She learned to smoke and to do the hoochie koochie. She guzzled booze and chanted:

> "Show me the way to go home.
> I'm tired and I wanna' go to bed.
> I had a little drink about an hour ago
> And it went right to my head."

She dreamed of Rudolph Valentino, the Sheik, and silently wished into her tent he'd creep. The Roaring Twenties was a glad time; a rag time, once in a lifetime, short time before and ebb time, the depression.

THE MASTODON SKELETON

An old couple, known as Grandma and Grandpa Dollar, often invited Willie and me a few days or over night visit in their home. A short hike, perhaps a mile, of walking the rails, and we would arrive there. A switch track, running parallel with the regular tracks, ended at our rear property line of the farm. One day as we hiked to the Dollars, a train had just added cars from the siding and was inching its way onto the main tracks, gradually picking up speed, Willie began running beside it. He called back that he was going to hop it. With tears streaming down face, I begged him not to. He merely laughed, quickened his pace, and continued running after the fast moving train. He finally grabbed hold of a ladder, attached to a boxcar, and pulled himself up on it. As I ran along the tracks, tripping and falling in the weeds, I yelled for him to jump off. I visualized him, mangled, mutilated and crushed under the rotating wheels. After what seemed an eternity he swung himself off and rolled down the incline of the rail bed. Between sobs and signs of relief, I swore I'd tell Hancel on him when we returned home.

The Dollars lived in a log cabin that had been built years earlier by Mr. Dollar's father. Feather ticks were used as mattresses on the beds we slept in. Giving a running jump, we would land on the bed and be pummeled deep into softness with the feather tick mounding around us.

To get to the privy I had to walk through a fenced in chicken yard. Mingled among the chickens was a mean old tom turkey. Every time I passed through his domain, he took after me. It ruffled its feathers, spread its tail, and trailed its wings on the ground, and literally attacked me. I was deathly afraid of it and I would delay a trip through the pen as long as I could. Finally I would persuade Willie to lure the creature away while I made the necessary trip. After the train-hopping incident he refused to

119

protect me unless I promised not to tell Hancel on him. Not having much choice, I reluctantly promised. As we entered the gate, he grabbed a stick and chased that bird to Kingdom come.

During those visits the old people regaled us with tales of the olden days as told to them by their parents. The told how Indians roamed the dense forest. How twining wild grape vines were, in some cases, almost as big around as the trees. How pigs were allowed to run loose; to subsist on nuts and wild berries, and how the owners notched their ears or branded them with numbers to identify them. In the fall they were rounded up and butchered for their meat. Grandpa Dollar often referred to a lake that once lay nearby, and how his father toiled to drain a vast swampy area where one could become mired in quicksand. Evidence of that swamp was still apparent during my school days when the skeleton of a prehistoric animal was discovered in that vicinity.

When the first big bone was unearthed, news spread about town. As more were discovered, speculation ran rampant. What could it be? Finally the diggings produced enough bones to warrant scientific examination. They were transported to Taylor University where each fragment was marked, labeled, and finally, bit-by-bit; an entire skeleton of a Mastodon was reassembled, and put on display at the University museum. School classes marched to the campus, on field trips, to view the huge beast's skeleton. Sadly, several years later, the museum caught on fire and the mastodon frame was destroyed.

At first the skeleton was the subject of many debates. Some said it wasn't a mastodon but merely the remains of an elephant that had escaped from the circus headquarters in Peru, Indiana. It was proven to be a mastodon.

Years later, on a return visit home, I tried to locate the old log cabin where the Dollars once lived. But I became confused. The cabin was gone. Where I remembered the cabin to be located there was a Purdue University Experimental Farm.

THE LOSE OF TWO LOVED ONES

The house next door, where Paula and her parents once lived was rented to the Green family, a couple with three sons. Mr. Green worked at a steady job in a neighboring town. Every Saturday, which was their father's payday, the boys anxiously awaited his homecoming. He always arrived bearing goodies and surprises. They would run to meet him and help carry packages. During the summer the family congregated on their front porch. Soon one of the boys would dash over and invite us to join them, to share in their treats, candy, peanuts, or perhaps a watermelon. Whatever it was, they usually shared it with us. When winter arrived, and we were confined inside, a bag of treats was often sent over to us. There were few paydays that we did not share in their bounty. Their boys were as much at home in our house as we were in theirs.

Harvey and Emma came periodically to check on their property. With each visit, Paula seemed frailer. Her vision had become so blurred all she could see was shapes and masses. She learned to read Braille. By merely running her fingertips over series of dots and dashes, raised on stark white paper, she could transpose them into words. She was mentally astute and keenly perceptive. She talked in high titters and laughed often. Although she could not run and play she was an entertaining playmate. On each visit she grew more fragile. In time a message arrived that she had died.

Harvey and Emma's visits became less frequent. Emma became reclusive and could hardly be persuaded to leave her home, so Harvey arrived alone. He said she was always asked him to be sure to stop and see how Hancel and the children were doing.

Hancel had barely reconciled herself to the news of Paula's death when a telegram arrived with the news that Aunt Vi had died. Her death was due to complication following the birth of a little daughter, which survived her by only a few days. Her thoughts turned immediately to Sadie. They attended her funeral together. She missed her sister cheerful demeanor, the sensible way she doled out advice; her witty personality and laughter. She missed the confidant who had sustained her during the long lonesome years following Louie's death. She grieved with a sorrow that would not abate. But she had learned, long ago, grieving would not lessen the pain. She entrenched Vi's memory deep within her mind. Although life went on as usual, she was left with an empty void in her heart.

It was once again time for the yearly crop to be harvested. That year it was navy beans. We picked the pods that had dried on the vines, carried them to the end of the rows, and dumped them into bushel baskets. Grandpa Mavis transferred them into burlap bags and loaded them on his wagon. He deposited Hancel's share in her coal shed, hanging suspended from hooks on the walls. She had to devise a method of turning the beans into hard cash, or equivalent. Once again the barter system came into play. It became a nightly ritual for her to drag in a bag of beans, sometimes two, for us to shell. Spreading newspapers on the kitchen floor she would dump a basket of beans in the middle of them, seat us cross-legged around the pile, and hand each of us a pie pan. As the beans pinged in the pan she read us stories. Since we didn't own many books, we quickly learned to check them out at the school library. When the stories became stale we memorized poems and entertained each other by reciting them aloud. My favorite poem was Horatio At The Bridge; but one I still remember is The Boy In Blue, as follows:

> Ho! Ho! Ho! Said the boy in blue
> I've got a big gun and I'm going to shot you.
> Oh, don't shot me said the little brown dog,
> Go down to the meadow and shot at a frog.
> I can't shot a frog. He won't stand still

He'll dive under the wheel of the mill.
Well! I won't stand still no more than a frog
So you can't shot me said the little brown dog.
I don't care said the boy in blue
I'll shot at a robin and bring him down to.
Do! Said the old cat that will be nice.
I'll crunch all his bones in a thrice.
The blue boy took aim, but he aimed not right.
Or like Cock Sparrow he shot in a fright.
The robin he missed, but he shot the old cat
And his grandma gave him a spanking for that!

RADIO VISION

When the beans were taken to the store to be traded for groceries, it was usually my chore to tote them there. I always carried a note listing the items, which Hancel wanted in exchange.

Most times it was ground beef, or hamburger. With twenty-five cents worth of ground meat Hancel could make a pot of soup by merely adding some of her home canned vegetables, a few chunks of potatoes and a fist full of rice. She could make a meatloaf; cook a pot of chili, or a pan of pasta. Every year Uncle Tony would bring us a long skinny package of spaghetti. Two bags of beans could be swapped for enough meat to make us the best treat of all, a hamburger sandwich. Just one. That was each one's share. Nothing tasted better than a pot of beans boiled with bacon with fluffy drop dumplings added, or beans with cornbread on the side.

The beans were traded to the huckster man and sold to friends and neighbors. When we collected for the weekly papers, we peddled dried beans to our customers. That bean crop lasted for two years, and the older they got the longer it took to cook them.

One day as I was shelling beans an old gentleman stopped to visit. I've forgotten the relationship. He may have been a friend of Williams, Hancel's father. Perhaps he was from the Friends Quarterly Meeting. He was from Richmond, Indiana, and was a Quaker and an inventor. He said that his first invention, made as a small boy, was a bean huller; a rotating wheel that when cranked removed the beans from the pods. He worked on it, secretly, for days in order to surprise his father. When he finally demonstrated the machine to him, his father laughed as he said, "Why, son, I can shell more beans by hand than your machine misses by a turn of the crank."

He said that although he was disappointed, it did not deter him from following his creative pursuits. He then informed me, "Woman was the first inventor. Eve, in the Garden of Eden, made an apron out of fig leaves. The loom, upon which cloth is woven, was invented by a woman." He went to the car and returned with a book and presented it to me. He autographed it C. Francis Jenkins, Aug./18/1932. It was a gift to me since I had just graduated from the eighth grade, and was ready to enter high school. Penciled below his name, in Hancel's handwriting, is noted "died 6/19/34."

C. Francis Jenkins invented the first motion picture projector, the Phantoscope. He opened the first motion picture theater at the cotton Exposition in Atlanta, Ga. Exhibits of a working plantation, with thatched roof dwellings, ignited. The fire quickly spread through the fairgrounds and destroyed many exhibitions, including the theater. The projector was destroyed, but he had another. Lacking funds, he acquired a partner, who later and without Jenkins knowledge, sold the patent to the Edison Manufacturing Company. Edison marketed it as the Edison Vitascope. However, the movie industry bestowed numerous citations on Jenkins for that invention.

Jenkins had a laboratory in Washington DC, where he made the first steam operated horseless carriage seen on the streets. He created the first paraffin coated milk carton and other food container, an automobile self-starter, ship-to-shore radio transmitter, and many other useful inventions. In January 1929, at the Indiana Home Coming Week, Jenkins announced that his first demonstration of Radio Vision had been a success. He predicted that, within a short time, ever home would have a. Radio Vision set. Radio Vision was the forerunner, or actually the first modern television. That was before we even owned a radio. That was over a half century ago, and that book is still one of my cherished possessions.

THE FAMILY PHOTO

The weather was very severe with many days reaching sub-zero temperatures. Although the boys now delivered the papers, Hancel often did it rather than expose them to the elements. She became ill and finally took to her bed with a high fever. She sent for Dr. Zimmerher, "You are completely exhausted and must stay in bed and rest. No more passing paper. Let your boy do it. You have pneumonia. Follow my instructions or you could die."

That night the high fever brought delirium. She called incoherently for Louie. By the next night she was more rational but worried about everything. She instructed me to go to her desk, unlock it, and bring her a bundle of letters, tied with a blue ribbon, that I would find there. When I returned with them, she read them, and tearfully bid me to burn them in the stove. I knew they were letters from James Allan, who now lived in Florida. Although separated by miles, they still corresponded for many years.

In later years, remembering back, I realized it was about the time that James Allan exited from her life that Hancel began using the phrase, "If it wasn't for you kids I'd get out of this town. I'd find a good man and get married." She was still an attractive young woman but would never wed another man, and have a life of her own, because her children's need always came first. She was, however only human in wishing for companionship. A memento I have cherished through the years is an article that appeared in our local paper under the caption "The Mirror." The heading states that the column is reserved for a worthy person in town; someone noted for business achievements, civic or spiritual worth. It is yellow with age and barely discernible in spots. It reads as follows:

"The Mirror reflects. Honors do not always belong to men. Praise is not always due to men in any community, nor should it always be confined to those most prominent in life. Often there is among us someone whose life is little noticed due to home duties, sacrifice, and other hindering conditions, but whose life shines many times brighter than those who appear constantly in our view.

Such a person, we believe, is Hancel Benedict. Some years ago Mr. Benedict died, leaving his family alone in the world with little to start life on. There were in the family several small children, wholly unable to care for themselves. Hancel went to work to raise and educate her children. Work was scarce but there was an opportunity, and she took it. Selling papers in a small town was a man's job, but leaving her children at home, she was to be seen daily, morning and evening, bravely traversing the streets, delivering her papers. This has continued for several years, until her children are now old enough to relieve her of the task. We have wondered sometimes, as others have done, how she was able to do it. But she did, and all through the years she has retained her place in the respect the community. She stands today as an example of motherhood and womanhood worthy of all our praise."

As the years passed, and I had children of my own, I, too, often wondered how she did it. She wore no halo and was only human, but I fully understand the phrase "my sainted mother." Especially when I recall how she had to contend with the antics of her children, — Like the time we had a family picture taken. For acquiring the required number of new customers for the Muncie Star, we won a certificate for a group picture, with a dozen prints, all for free.

Hancel washed and ironed our best bibs-and-tuckers, especially the boys white starched shirts. She sent us all for haircuts, and exerted every effort to make us look our best. As the time neared for our ride to arrive, she admonished us to hurry and get dressed. Willie had just slipped into his wrinkle free, freshly ironed white shirt and Joseph was shining his shoes. Willie uttered some remark that displeased Joseph. With the blackened shoe brush in hand, Joe took off after Willie, and caught him. Try as he would, Willie was unable to escape Joe's vengeance. He smeared shoe blackening all over his face. Luckily no polish was transferred to the shirt. Willie was in tears. As jabs and pokes continued, dissension reigned. For Hancel it was a battle of nerves all day.

Another time Joseph and Willie were playing, rough housing and scuffing around. Willie dashed into the house with Joseph in pursuit. As Willie entered the door, banging it shut, Joseph crashed into the door and broke the glass. The next day one of the boys threw a stone at the other. He missed his mark, and the rock smashed through the parlor window shattered slivers of glass all over the room.

The next day a neighbor girl and I had a difference of opinion over something. As she angrily ran home, she taunted me by calling me Dago. I chased her all the way to her front porch, where thinking she was safe, she continued calling me names. I picked up a rock and pelted it at her. I missed her but broke the window behind her. Hancel was forced to pay for three windows, all in one week, out of her limited budget.

Only the Lord preserved her sanity! How she managed to feed, cloth and educate us; raise us to maturity; and love us in the process, still remains a mystery.

THE DEPRESSION

People began talking about the depression, about hard times, but our life went on as usual. Although Hancel had a hard time making ends meet, as she said, we had it better than many families. She worked when most men had no job. Besides the paper route, working as a domestic, washing and ironing, that she finally discontinued, we always had produce to barter. We had fresh vegetables from our garden, and the chicken she raised supplied us with both eggs and meat. Still, she devised another method of earning income. She became the agent for the California Perfume Company and Dr. Sayman's Products. When she ran short of funds, she would say, "Julia, take the sample case and go see if you can sell something. Your sister needs a new pair of shoes." I became adept at peddling products; an original Avon Lady.

I learned just where, and to whom, I could make a sale. One elderly lady was a cinch to buy a can of talcum powder every time I stopped. She always smelled good and looked like a cross between a white bunny and a marshmallow. Aromatic odors and spicy sweet smell that wafted from her kitchen whet my appetite. She loved to bake and usually gave me a treat. Before departing I managed, not only to sell the talcum powder, I promoted the sale of a bottle of perfume, or toilet water. The spicy aromas emanating from her kitchen, coupled with her baking enthusiasm, inspired me to return later with the Dr. Sayman's products; vanilla, pure vanilla with a bean in every bottle; salves, soaps and spices. I would rattle off a spiel of how nothing was better for washing hair than Dr. Sayman's soap. It was as good as shampoo and not as costly. Besides vanilla I also sold lemon, almond, coconut and maple extract. Her husbands' love of maple guaranteed a sale.

Another favorite customer was a plum and peppery maiden lady whose hair was always kinky from wrapping it in strands of rags. Everyone in town knew she had a new, out of town, beau that he visited every Wednesday and Saturday nights, and Sunday he spent the entire day at her house. Neighbors didn't miss much and they talked a lot. The sweet old soul primped and dressed in the latest fashions. It was easy for me to persuade her that a certain scent of perfume would enhance the romance; or that the right shade of blush would complement her skin, and that Dr. Sayman's soap would highlight her hair. But the cosmetic she most desired was a wrinkle remover. "Do you have anything that will remove the crow's feet from the corner of my eyes?" Of course I did! Dr. Sayman's astringent was just the right stuff. It was sure to work wonders. A repeat sale was assured when the bottle was empty.

It was apparent that the depression was in full swing when Mr. Green lost his job. For a man who had always brought home the bacon, one who had always provided stability for his family, to suddenly find himself out of a job, and with the knowledge that the prospects of finding another did not look good, it was a crushing blow. Finding no job locally, or in the neighboring towns, he took to the road seeking employment.

He was only one of thousands who swelled the ranks of jobless, at a time when unemployment benefits were unheard of. Although he searched far and wide, no steady work was forthcoming. An occasional letter brought a small remittance to sustain his family. Finally, Ms. Green tearfully confided to Hancel that all her boys had for supper the previous night was a mustard sandwich, and she didn't know where their next meal was coming from. Hancel moved her coal oil stove out into the yard, between the two houses. She salvaged a table from the shed, and every day, for the remainder of the summer, she cooked something that would feed both families. The bean crop with a bit of bacon, and a pan of corn bread often topped the menu. On Sundays she killed a chicken and made noodles.

Often it was a pan of pasta, or a pot of soup. Sometimes it was merely biscuits and gravy, or jelly. Whatever she had she shared.

After weeks of fruitless searching for work, Mr. Green returned home and moved his family back home with his wife's family. The house stood empty for several months before Harvey dismantled it, piece by piece. He layered the lumber in piles; the windows and doors in another, and stacked the concrete blocks. A few days later a truck arrived to haul it all away. The materials were sold for whatever price they would bring. Eventually the property reverted to the county for back taxes owed.

Another calamity that indicated hard times had arrived was the disappearance of a neighbor man, the head of a large household. With seven children to feed and cloth, he was barely holding on. When the arrival of another set of twins boosted the number to nine souls, the overwhelmed father simply vanished. The wife beset with unpaid bills and wailing babies soon packed their meager belongings and disappeared from town.

Another sign that the depression was escalating was the number of hoboes who rode the freight trains, and crossed the fields to knock on our door seeking a hand out. Hancel never turned one away. First she would give them a pan of water, soap and a towel, so the could wash. This was usually as greatly appreciated as the food. Sometimes all she could give them was a fried egg sandwich, a cup of tea, or a glass of water. But she always shared with those she considered less fortunate than herself.

Every year, like the harbinger of spring, one particular hobo showed up. As soon as the earth warmed he would arrive. Probably smelling him, the neighborhood dogs were the first to announce his presence. Every stray in town was on hand to welcome and pursue him. Their chorus of yelps and barks attracted boys of all ages. They quickly spread the word that "Wooly Woody's back in town!"

Woody was a sight to behold! He was clad in coats of mis-matched lengths, three and four layers deep. Like the Biblical Joseph, Woody wore coats of many colors. Long tailed coats hung below shorter ones, and from the padded effect one surmised that many lay unseen beneath the long and the short of them. He was short in stature with snow-white hair and a bushy beard. His shoes were scuffed and holes were visible in their soles. A battered old hat sat perched at a jaunty angle atop his mass of hair.

After attracting the boys attention he would produce, from the recesses of his many pockets, a harmonic or a Jew's harp and proceed to play a couple of tunes as he shuffled his feet in a hobo jig. After a sizeable group was assembled, he pulled out a number of slingshots and offered them for sale. He also sold popguns that he had hand carved out of wood.

If a boy was lucky enough to have a dime, a sale was consummated there and then. If not, Woody would wait until a boy dashed home for funds. He was in no hurry. If the items didn't sell for a dime, the price was quickly reduced to a nickel as a bargain between friends. He wasn't averse to taking pennies, if pennies were all a lad had.

When all sales were completed he whistled a couple of tunes to indicate the performance was over. Then with the proceeds of the sales firmly clutched in his hand, he headed for the grocery store. He usually bought a ring of baloney and a bag of crackers from the barrel. If money allowed, he bought a cold sarsaparilla. Most often he finished his feast at the drinking fountain. Leftover goodies were stashed in one of his pockets before he sought the shade of a tree under which to take a nap. Since I was a girl, I was not allowed to follow Woody around town. If he didn't happen to stop near our home, I had to rely on a secondhand version of his visits.

I JOINED THE BAND

The school was organizing a high school band. As a junior high student I could enroll. Students were asked to bring their parents to a meeting to discuss the possibilities of purchasing instruments on the installment plan. I knew that we could never afford an instrument outright. I also knew Hancel would never agree to an installment plan. If we didn't have money to purchase something, we did without. Seeing my enthusiasm, she agreed to attend the meeting. She wanted her children to have every opportunity that other students had.

After a conference with the bandmaster, she announced to me that there was no way we could afford a new musical instrument. I should reconcile myself to the situation and put the idea out of my mind. A few days later, as she worked at a house-cleaning job, the subject of the band and my desire to join it arose. The lady of the house had a grown son who no longer lived at home, but who had left behind an E Flat Alto saxophone. She would gladly sell it to conserve space. When Hancel arrived home and relayed the news to me. I rushed right over to check it out.

Julia in the band

It was a brass instrument. Everyone else has a silver one. The wooden, leather covered case was so heavy I could hardly carry it. I didn't care. It could have been a lop-sides pink polka dotted tuba in a tin box! Anything just so I could join the band. How she ever managed was beyond me, but Hancel made a deal and I joined the band. Joining the band opened up a whole new world for me. I could attend basketball games, take trips, play in concerts, march in parades, and participate in special events, all free, by merely being a band member.

On Memorial Day we marched to the cemetery, which was probably a three mile round trip. At that time there were three old Civil War soldiers still alive in our town. They marched along with us, but accepted rides back. The ceremonies were held in the section of the cemetery reserved for veterans of the Civil War and World War I. The march was repeated on the Fourth of July when the sweltering heat made the journey seem twice as far. When the rites were concluded one old Civil War veteran always gave each of us a silver dollar. The old hearse that my grandfather made, years ago, was usually a part of the parade, allowing me to brag to my friends that he had made it.

After one Memorial Day parade, as the players disbanded, a lady came up to me and asked if I was little Julia Benedict, now growing up. She told me of sitting on her front porch and watching Hancel, my two older brothers, and me, as we walked by her house on the first Memorial Day after my father died. We each carried a bouquet of flowers so she knew that we were on our way to put them on our father's grave. By the time her vivid account was finished, I was near tears. When I related the conversation to Hancel, she confirmed that we had, indeed, walked that long walk years ago.

I never knew how Hancel was able to buy the saxophone. Neither did I know what ever happened to the silver loving cup that my father won in the long ago dance contest. Shortly after I acquired my instrument, as I dusted the pedestal upon which the trophy always sat, I noticed it was gone. It had always sat on that pedestal beside a picture of him - standing beside a pedestal. When I asked Hancel about it she said she must have stored it away somewhere. Years later I wondered, could she have sold the loving cup to purchase my saxophone for me.

THE BANKS CLOSE

Even though hard times worsened we were able to save money for a new radio. Hancel deposited the money in the bank. A few nights later she wrote an order to Sears and Roebucks, through the catalog, and intended to purchase a money order the next day. By morning newspaper headlines announced the banks had closed. The radio money was gone, as was her small hoard of cash reserved for emergencies.

Gone was the widow's mite, along with the wealth of the rich and mighty, the savings of the hard working farmers, as were the funds of the butcher, the baker, and the local church funds. The Merchants bank eventually repaid depositors in the form of script; vouchers that could be redeemed at local stores and business establishments.

Once again we started saving pennies, nickels, and dimes; coins that were allotted as kids share of the proceeds for helping deliver newspapers. Finally, we amassed enough to order a radio. We no longer had to listen to second versions of Jack Armstrong, the All American Boy, as related to us by our friends. We dashed home from school to hear it on our brand new radio. Besides Jack we listened to The Shadow, Lamont Cranston, as he posed the eerie question, "What evil lurks in the hearts of men? Only the shadow knows!" Rudy Valley crooned I'm Just A Vagabond Lover, and Kate Smith sang When the Moon comes Over the Mountain.

Even though, for many, it was not true, the lyric most often heard was LIFE IS JUST A BOWL OF CHERRIES. It was warbled as headlines screamed STOCK MARKET CRASHES, and there was talk of Black Tuesday. (Or was it Thursday?) Another song lamented, "Once I built a railroad; made it run — Brother can you spare a dime? Business tycoons, once high up the ladder of success, joined the multitude of unemployed standing in bread lines. They sold pencils and apples in order to eat. The number of men knocking on our back door increased daily.

One day a man rapped on the door. Thinking he was another hobo, Hancel went through her customary routine of offering him a pan of water, soap, and a towel. She told him to sit down and she would bring him something to eat. The man began to cry as he asked, "Why, Hancel, don't you know me?"

Then she recognized him; our old neighbor, Mr. Green. The man who always shared treats with us on payday. A man who was always neat and clean, who walked tall and proud. He was emaciated and haggard. His cheeks were sunken and hollow, and he needed a shave. His cloths looked like the garb of a scarecrow. Tired, and obviously ill, he began to weep. He sobbed out tales of traveling the country. Of walking and begging for rides; how he rode the rails in search of employment.

It had all be for naught. He was returning to his family broken in spirit because he could no longer support them. Hancel opened her heart to him, as well as her home. She wept with him. After he had washed, which he said he hadn't done for days, She prepared food for him. As he ate he related the plight of other men looking for work. Men he had encountered in freight cars. In some cases they weren't even men, but mere boys. Girls, too, dressed as boys also rode the boxcars. Men and boys, old and young, all transients following the warmth of the sun, as he said, "At least it was better to be warm than cold." He told of food riots in the cities, and how the Red Cross handed out food. Finding one of their centers was like finding a pot of gold at the end of a rainbow. For many it was the salvation that kept body and soul alive. He finally laid down to rest, slept the clock around. He ate again before starting the last lap of his journey home to rejoin his family. A few months later we were saddened to receive a letter from his wife informing us of his death. - Only one, of many, victims of the depression.

Despite hard times, the Marion Chronicle held a contest for signing up new customers. The prize was a Thanksgiving turkey. We won one! Grandma Sadie arrived by train to spend the holidays with us. — And life was, indeed, like a bowl of cherries!

One night while Hancel was off attending some ladies meeting, Joseph invited a bunch of buddies in to play cards. He knew he shouldn't have friends in during her absence, much less to be playing cards. He warned his friends that the game had to end before she arrived home. Knowing this, boys casually commented on what he would do if she caught them red-handed. One said, "If I hear her coming, I'll beat it out the front door." Another said, "I'll toss all the cards in the stove." Each expounded on the other.

Willie would not join in their game. He sat silently listening to their schemes. After a few minutes, unnoticed, he crept out the front door. Treading nosily, he went around the house, ascended the porch, and stomped his feet, as if knocking the snow off them, as Hancel would before entering the house. You never heard such shuffling of feet and banging of chairs as they hid the cards and tidied the room. Then, realizing Willie had tricked them, each took a turn at playfully pummeling him. Even so they made a quick departure.

One day as Hancel walked past the barbershop, the friendly barber beckoned to her. He said, "Hancel, after I finished cutting Willie's hair yesterday, he asked me how much a haircut cost. He took change out of his pocket, counted it and said, from now on he would pay for his haircut."

"He must of used money earned yesterday picking strawberries"

"Yes, he said he earned three cents a quart. One certainly has to admire that boy."

"Yes, I am. I guess you've noticed that he is a very sensitive boy, a proud boy."

"Yes, and I've also notices that he get both of those traits from his mother."

OUR FATHER'S BLUE SERGE SUIT

One day, as Hancel was ironing cloths, Joseph entered the house and hurried directly to the bedroom. When he came out he was carrying his father's blue serge suit. Hancel had meticulously sewn it inside a bag, made from a sheet, in order to protect it from moths and dust. As Joseph unwrapped the garment, Hancel asked, "What are you doing with your father's suit?"

"I'm going to give it to my friend Clyde. He has an interview for a job tomorrow and the only thing he has to wear is a pair of bib overalls. My Dad would want him to have this suit so he would have a better chance of getting that job."

Hancel, on the verge of ordering him to return the suit to the closet, hesitated a moment, thinking. She finally said, "You're right. Your father would give him the suit if he were here. It has hung in the closet long enough. Take it to Clyde and wish hum luck."

The next evening, returning from his job interview, dressed in his newfound finery, Clyde stopped to show off how nice he looked. Hancel, dirty after toiling in the garden, and with the children being absent, had stripped and was bathing at the kitchen sink. In his excitement, Clyde burst through the door without knocking. Hancel quickly grabbed a towel to cover her nudity, as Clyde beat a hasty retreat. Hancel called, "Don't you ever enter my house again without knocking, young man."

"I won't Mrs. Benedict. I just wanted to tell you the good news. I got the job. I'm now an employed shoe salesman. Without the suit that Joe gave me, I know I wouldn't have been hired. Thanks."

As she listened to his receding footstep, Hancel thought, "The trousers were a bit short. If I had known, I could have lengthened them. I could have faced them."

Willie disappeared. He did not come home for dinner. Darkness fell and he still had not returned. Hancel sent Joseph to search for him. He made the rounds of Willie's favorite haunts and checked with several of his buddies. Willie could not be located. Hancel was frantic. When morning came, and he still had not returned home, she went to the marshal's office to report him missing. He was gone for three days before the marshal reported that the Kentucky police had picked him up, along with a friend who had also been reported missing. They were escorting them back to Indiana.

Hancel was so relieved to her son safely home that she meted out no punishment, except to scold him, and make him promise to never run away again. Willie said that they only wanted to have an adventure, to see a bit of the world.

With little or no money in their pockets, the boys hitched rides. When they were hungry they stopped at farmhouses and asked to do chores for their meals. Or at a restaurant where they washed dishes in exchange for food. Finally a friendly proprietor, after questioning the boys as to where they lived, suspected they were run-a-ways and called the police. Throughout their lives those two boys remained best buddies. They were basketball and baseball teammates, and when they started dating, they double dated.

The friend, Kenny, lived with his grandparents on a farm. He helped his granddad around the farm and earned a weekly allowance. When his granddad mentioned that the next-door farmer needed a boy to help him occasionally, Kenny relayed the information to Willie. Willie was hired to do chores a few evenings each week and usually on Saturday.

As the boys rambled around the acreage an old abandoned Model T Ford, hidden in the weeds, almost obscured from view, caught their eyes. Upon inquiring of the old farmer if the car was for sale, he answered, "If you boys can get that flivver running, I will sell it to you."

Each boy started saving his money. Their spare time was consumed with working on the automobile. They tinkered under the hood, and following the advise of a friendly garage mechanic, they made repairs and adjustments. They painted and primed it, and to the amazement of the old farmer, when they turned the crank the motor pinged, sputtered and finally purred to perfection. Pooling their money they came up with twenty-five dollars. The farmer accepted it as the sale price of the car. They christened it Ananias, and proudly cruised about town showing it off to their friends. Their first trip in their car turned out to be a sad experience. A trip that both boys later agreed they wished they had never taken.

It started out as a happy jaunt to Marion, Indiana to take in a movie. When they arrived in town, a crowd milling around the courthouse square attracted their attention. With curiosity, they gravitated to the area to check out activities. To their horror, they found two bodies hanging suspended from the trees. They listened to the story of how three young black men had, supposedly, robbed and killed a white man and assaulted his female companion as they were parked in a dark remote area. Two of the men had just been lynched by the white mob. They had been beaten and their bodies were mutilated. The agitated mass of onlookers where screaming for another young black man, confined in jail, to be released to them for similar treatment. Willie, said, "I got sick at my stomach and vomited right there."

Having been reared by the tenets of the Friends church "red or yellow, black or white, all are precious in his sight" Willie considered it a revolting atrocity, and a terrifying experience. One they both wished they had never chanced upon. They lost all interest in seeing a movie, and returned home immediately. He was still unnerved as he related the tale to us. He was happy when newspaper accounts told how the remaining young man had been whisked away to safety, escaping a similar fate.

MY LAST SUMMER SPENT AT UNCLE TONY

The summer I graduated from the eighth grade was the last summer I spent at Uncle Tony's. Angie had entered the convent to become a nun. The two younger boys were attending the seminary, before becoming ordained priest. Only an older cousin, Louie, remained at home to help till the farm and to market the produce. Boys from the city were hired to clean the onions, bunch the radishes, pick green beans, to polish the tomatoes and pack them in baskets. I no longer helped with these chores.

Produce that did not sell at the market was taken to Cousin Frank's store to be sold. One day as Louie pulled up in front of the store to deliver a load of vegetables a man was fleeing down the sidewalk with a policeman in close pursuit. As the man came abreast of Louie's truck, he tossed a half filled liquor bottle through the window. It landed on the seat beside Louie. After capturing the fugitive, the policeman returned and told Louie, although he saw the bottle being thrown into the truck, due to Indiana's Bone Dry Law of 1925, it was illegal to have even an open liquor bottle in a vehicles, and Louie might be called upon to testify in court.

When Louie arrived home and related the events to Uncle Tony, he became excited. He was sure the revenue men would come and search their premises and find all the paraphernalia used in making homebrew. They would find the grape and dandelion wine, not to mention some of the stronger stuff kept strictly for medicinal purposes. In this agitated state of mind, Uncle Tony decided he would conceal the incriminating evidence until after the trial. Louie laughed at the idea. He chided his father and ridiculed the scheme, all to no avail. No amount of persuasion could dissuade Uncle Tony. Every bottle and crock must be cached away. He began to contrive a hiding

143

place for the illegal liquors. Finally, he came up with the perfect place. Even the cagey T Men wouldn't be able to ferret out the location.

Their home sat on a slight hill. The lane sloped from the barn and garage, down the hill and around the house. It rambled over a small creek and continued on to finally emerged onto a county road. It was probably a distance of three-fourths of a mile to the highway, and the creek laid half way between the two. A few feet beyond the creek stood a large brown manure pile. It was under this odious and steamy mound, that attracted blue buzz flies, grubby worms and scavenger birds that Uncle Tony decided to stash the evidence. No amount of begging, bribing or sarcasm could change his mind. Not even the suggested aromatic, newly filled hayloft would do. The manure pile was the place he had decided upon, and the manure pile it would be!

Crocks and hoses, bottles, caps and capper, and everything connected with booze making were packed into crates, barrels, boxes, and canvas bags. All was loaded on the wagon and carted to the creek and buried under the manure pile. Carrie Nations and her hatchet welding crew would have had a hay day! For days Uncle Tony's disposition was as foul as the dung heap under which his daily brew was hidden.

Needless to say, it was all in vain. The Revenuers never came. All the barrel, bottles, and liquid beverages were restored to their usual place. Life returned to normal. The brewing continued, and once again I carried the pitcher of foamy beer to the field for Uncle Tony to wet his whistle.

With only Louie remaining at home, I turned to him for companionship. I tagged him around as he crooned popular songs of the day; Carolina Moon, Sweet Georgia Brown, and The Sheik of Ar-rab-ie. To me he was Rudolph Valentino, Douglas Fairbanks Jr. and Apollo all rolled into one. I never returned to the farm after that summer. Perhaps I was growing up.

AUNT MAUDIE REAPPEARS

In 1932 I entered high school. I was a freshman! I had caught up with Willie. Joseph was a senior. Cosmetics that I sold from my sample case began to appeal to me. I experimented with lipstick and rouge. If I applied too much Hancel made me wash it off, or Willie called me a freak. I did the armpit test and bought a bottle of Odor-o-no. I made flax seed wave set and tried new hairstyles, even a permanent.

I had never owned a new coat, only hand-me-downs. I saved money earned for delivering papers, selling products, and from baby setting job. I bought my first new coat, a blue cloth chinchilla that cost seven dollars. (It was then that Hancel related the tale of the coat she bought year ago.) I accumulated more cash and bought an Empress Eugenie hat. It was adorned with a plume that curled around my face. I thought I was the cat's meow!

I began to notice boys. Boys began to notice me! The one who most took my fancy was a fellow band member. He soon asked if he could walk me home from practice. As he reached to pick up my saxophone case, the weight of it pulled him over. I took pity on him and carried it myself. His small stature had earned him the nickname of Peanuts. When Willie disparagingly referred to him as Peeny-Weeny, all sex appeal vanished. I gave Prince Charming the gate!

Girls who once gathered at a maiden lady's house to play authors began congregating at one another's homes to dance. The country had survived the Charleston and the Black Bottom. We practiced the two-step and the fox trot. We shagged and Shuffled Off To Buffalo to the popular tunes that blared forth from the radio. The speak-easies, nightclubs and roadhouses had ushered in the era of the big bands that were making a name for them-selves. Hancel did not approve of dancing. It was not so

145

much that she disapproved. But rather, that ours was a small town, church oriented, and those who did not sanction dancing would talk.

Julia

No one had money for dates. We met together for fun and games; played tennis at the campus, and took long hikes. If one of the boys had permission to use the family car, we all piled in and rode to a neighboring town, Marion or Hartford City, to see a movie. On pleasant nights we sat around campfires and

concocted parodies -like the following sang to the tune of Glow
Worm:

> In the moonlight, glitter, glitter
> Stood a figure, slimmer, slimmer.
> Her teeth were false and her hair peroxide
> And in the moonlight she looked cross-eyed.
> The ruffles on her petticoat, blowing in the breezes
> Scraped like sandpaper on her knee-es—The rest is
> forgotten.

We didn't go steady as couples did a few years later. We
were just friends having a good time together. Occasionally a
couple paired off in a dark corner, but that was taboo, and
frowned upon.

With the depression in full swing, the county found it
difficult to keep schools open and operational.   Only by
consolidating the two Jefferson Township schools, Upland and
Matthews, were both able to remain open.   Teachers taught
classes in one school in the morning and traveled to the other
town for afternoon sessions. With school activities combined we
made many new friend, especially boy friends.   We soon
discovered which teacher would play Cupid by carrying notes
back and forth.

I was sixteen when I had my first real date. Accompanied by
another couple, my date and I were taking in the Blackford
County Fall fair. We had ridden the Ferris wheel, observed the
bearded lady and Pygmy fire-eater. We had consumed hot dogs,
cotton candy and popcorn. We pitched balls and played games
before starting down the freeway, seeking new adventures.

We followed the sound of the barker's voice as he
announced, "Come one, come all. Feast your eyes on our lovely
Beauties. See how the serpent tempted Eve into eating the apple
in the Garden of Eden. A free five minute show is about to
begin." A crowd was assembled around a wooden platform in

front of a huge tent. We pushed our way through the throng to the first row. Soon, four scantily clad showgirls pranced out of the tent and ascended the stage. I felt nervous watching a girlie show, especially accompanied by my first important boy friend. Between wiggles and catcalls, the girls took their positions in line, as the barker called, "And here is our star attraction, Little Eve straight from the Garden of Eden." Exiting the tent, and gyrating toward the stage was a sleek blond with a huge snake draped around her neck. She slunk into line mid-way between the other girls, adjusted the snake to her shoulders, threw back her head and flashed a big smile. -

Horror! Do my eyes deceive me? That can't be Aunt Maudie up there on the stage with a snake coiled around her body! I suddenly felt sick. I dashed from the area with my friends in pursuit wanting to know what ailed me. I explained that I must have eaten too much cotton candy and hot dogs, coupled with the twirling rides, I felt ill.

Arriving at home, I recited the events of the evening to Hancel. Her indignant response was, "Impossible! Aunt Maudie a carnival dancer? She would never be performing in a carnival, much less with a snake around her neck. It was just someone who looked like her!"

At the breakfast table the next morning, directing his question, or remark, to no one in particular Joseph said, "Guess who I saw appearing as a Hoochie Koochie dancer at the carnival last night?" To his surprise Hancel answered, questioningly, "Aunt Maudie?" He had watched the performance to the very end and could verify that it was, indeed, Aunt Maudie. - To my knowledge, that was the last time any of us ever saw Aunt Maudie. ——

Projecting the tale ahead many years. Sometime in the 60s, my husband and I had acquired our first recreational vehicle and were traveling to the west coast. We had invited Hancel to accompany us. Finding ourselves in Oregon we decided to look up Uncle Mike.

Hancel carried her address book in her purse. Perhaps she had anticipated the search. We drove to Mike's last known address. My husband went to the door, and after assuring himself that the man who responded to his knock was really Uncle Mike, he said, "There's someone out in the car who would like to talk to you."

A rather short, rotund man with white hair approached us. He looked like a refugee from a Leprechaun colony. He peered at us but registered no sign of recognition. I wanted to hug him for old time sake, but time had made us strangers. Extending my hand, I said, "I know you won't remember me. I'm Louie's daughter."

With a puzzled look on his face, he asked, "Louie who?"

What did I expect? His brother had been dead for over forty years. Uncle Mike had not seen us since he had left Indiana. When he finally realized that it was Hancel standing before him, all he could say, over and over again, was, "So this is Hancel? That lovely lady. I never thought I'd see you again." Somewhere along life's path, he had become a holy roller and was prone to quote scripture. We could establish no common interest, and cut our visit short. —No mention was made of Maudie.

A TRAGIC ACCIDENT

Word came from Hancel's brother, Jay that his toddler son had died as the result of a tragic accident. Aunt Dorothy, Jay's sister, was visiting them at their rural home near Fort Wayne, Indiana. Like most county homes of the era, it lacked many modern conveniences. In preparation for washing the supper dishes, Dorothy had put a teakettle of water on the stove to heat. After a few minutes she poured boiling water from the kettle into a dishpan that was sitting on the kitchen table. As she turned to replace the kettle on the stove, she failed to notice that the toddler son had wondered into the room. The child reached up, grabbed the edge of the tablecloth, tipped the pan, and spilt scalding water over his entire body.

Hearing the child's screams, his father grabbed him and ripped off his diaper, which was the only garment he wore on that hot summer day. The lower part of his body had been badly burned. His father rushed him to the hospital but all attempt to save his life proved futile. Within a few days he died of uremic poisoning. Needless to say, the family was devastated, especially Aunt Dorothy. No amount of persuasion could convince her that she was not to blame. She crucified herself needlessly.

Hancel attended the funeral and wake. After the funeral friends and family met at Jay's house to visit. As was often the case, in those days, such an occasion was the only contact family members had with each other for years at a stretch. It was a time of sorrow, but of reunion. She returned home weepy and low in spirit for days, reliving sorrowful memories of Vi and Louie.

In an endeavor to shake her melancholia, I related an incident that happen one summer when I was visiting at Uncle Jay and Aunt Mabel. Their two little sons were probably about five and three years old at the time. One day they both disappeared from their play yard and I was sent to find them. I finally found them in the garage busily pounding nails into the tires of Uncle Jay's brand new car. I led them into the house and reported the situation to Aunt Mabel. She dashed out to survey the damage. Luckily, the boys did not have the strength to hammer the nails deep into the tires. They were easily removed, but Aunt Mabel thought it best to keep the prank a secret from Uncle Jay.

I chattered on about how Mabel's mother, as a member of the Mennonite church, always wore a tiny lace cap on her head, and usually wore long, drab colored dresses. In explaining why the unusual garb Mabel told me that, like the Pilgrims, the sect had carried their customs and religion to America, but from Germany, years ago. Many had settles in the Fort Wayne area. She added that they were somewhat like the Amish in their ways. Of course I had to ask who the Amish where. Her best explanation was they clung to the old ways, and didn't believe in having modern conveniences, automobiles and such. She said she had been raised according to their customs but as she grew older she began to resist them, especially when it came to the matter of dress. She couldn't catch a beau that way! As she went out into the workplace, and married, she learned to like the modern contraptions too much to abide by their rules.

As I related this to Hancel, I injected the fact that between being brought up by the tenets of the Friends church; exposed to beliefs of the Catholic church when visiting Uncle Tony's; and then to learn about the Mennonites and the Amish, religion could become downright confusing as to which was the right one. It seemed some were more concerned with what to wear, what to drive or ride than in the teachings of the Bible. In a short time my chatter had Hancel laughing, and in stoical manner, she put aside her sorrow and life went on.

WILLIE' CHRISTMAS BOX

Willie rarely conceded that girls actually existed until he suddenly began to pay attention to one particular little blonde, named Helen. Being proud of my handsome brother, I thought he could do better by picking one without freckles. In fact, I knew a couple of girls who would give anything for even a cross-eyed peek from Willie. But Willie had eyes only for Helen. Willie was smitten! His school class was having a Christmas party. He invited her to attend with him, and she accepted. It would be his first date. He saved money to buy her something special for Christmas.

On the night of the party, he slicked his hair and shined his shoes. He donned his best sweater, wore a tie, and topped it off with his cap. With this perched atop his head at a jaunty angle, he departed the house with a wink and a whistle.

When he knocked on her door her father, responding to the rap, opened it. At Willie's greeting, he informed him, "Helen won't be going to the party with you. No daughter of mine is going anywhere with a dammed Dago kid. Stay away from Helen if you know what's good for you." With that remark he slammed the door. Willie was stunned!

He arrived home dejected and near tears. As he tried to hold back the tears, he vented his anger by hurling the wrapped gift he had intended to give to Helen. It collapsed on the floor with a crash. I retrieved it and handed it to him.

"Keep it. I never want to see it again!"

I removed the wrappings and found a beautiful metal jewelry box. The hinge was broken. (It still is, and I have cherished that box for over a half a century)

As Flancel listened to Willie's recitation of the evening's events, it was hard for her to hold back the tears. "Will my children ever be able to escape the stigma that narrow minded people attach to them just because their father happened to have been born in Italy? No one ever mentions your Scotch-Irish heritage from my family. Your father was a far better person than the bigot who did this to you, Willie. I wonder what your lives would have been like if I had not married Louie. If I had married one of a different nationality you kids would not have been called Dago all the time."

I couldn't believe my ears! She loved and respected Louie. She was proud of him. I remember Aunt Vi once telling her that she was justified in her pride, after Hancel repeated an opinion that Dr. Zimmer had voiced saying, "If Louie had lived he would own half the town by now."

As children, and even later, the name Dago plagued us. I recall an incident, years later. As I was being introduced to a woman, she reminded me that we had gone to school together. She added, "Yes, but I didn't like you."

Stunned by her candor, I asked, "Why was that. Why didn't you like me?"

"Because you once threw my new hat in a mud puddle."

"Now what ever made me do a thing like that?"

"I called you Dago."

I laughed, "That would do it! In those days Dago was a fighting word to me. It no longer bothers me. In fact, I'm proud of my Italian heritage."

HAPPY DAYS AND NEW DEALS

With the election of FDR we began to hear "prosperity is just around the corner, Happy Days Are Here Again, and talk of a New Deal." Unemployed men were put to work on the WPA, Works Project Administration. Their first project in our town was the construction of new out-houses, derisively referred to as Roosevelt's Palaces. One out of three homes in the US had no inside facilities, or bathroom until the forties, or after the war. It was hoped the new sanitary facilities would contain germs and slow the spread of dreaded polio that had crippled FDR. The buildings were constructed on cement, with concrete tanks, with a screened window, vented air pipe, and two seats. I'll never comprehend why it had two seats, since no one ever wanted company when making a necessary trip down the garden path. The new privies cost fifteen dollars.

The WPA workers became the object of good-natured jokes. Cartoonist lampooned them with sketches of idle workers leaning on their shovels. But those WPA jobs were the salvation for many families. If the project had been initiated before Mr. Green was force to take to the road seeking work, he might have remained alive longer.

Boys quit school to join the newly organized CCC, Civilian Conservation Corps. Young men from the age of seventeen to twenty-five were paid a salary of thirty dollars a month for joining a job corp. Five dollars was allotted to the boy and the balance was sent home to parents to help support their families. When Joseph tried to persuade Hancel to let him join, she quickly let him know that it was more important for him to stay in school. She had managed to support us for years, and would continue to do so.

In our town, the CCC boys dug up bricks from the old bumpy and wavy streets. They leveled the ground, cleaned the old bricks, replaced the broken ones with new ones, and re-laid them. They were responsible for the construction of many state and national parks and campgrounds. They built roads, planted trees, and performed tasks necessary in preserving and protecting our natural resources, such as caves, rivers and lakes, and other natural wonders.

Another plan instituted to help the needy, the largest segment of the population of the US, was the distributions of surplus food. A truck appeared regularly, driving up and down city streets passing out commodities, fruits and vegetables that would have spoiled for lack of purchasing power since no one had any money.

At first Hancel was reluctant to receive this free food, considering it to be charity. But when it became apparent that almost the entire population of the town lined up to receive the free bounty, she concluded that her children were as deserving as the next one, so she followed suite.

One thing about the depression, rich, or once rich, and poor alike was in the same boat financially. Few escaped the adverse effects. Looking back, I think we had it better than many families. The commodity most appreciated was the canned meat, chunks of lean beef swimming in its juices. With a batch of homemade noodles simmered in broth, it became the basis of a sumptuous feast.

When money was available it's purchasing power was strong and inflation unheard of. Every Saturday I walked to a nearby farm and bought a quart of whipping cream for twenty-five cents. Fifteen cents bought a quart of cottage cheese, or smearcase, as Hancel called it. Sunday evening meals consisted of Jello mixed with fruit, topped with mounds of whipped cream, and home made cake; made from scratch.

Instituted as a theater and writers project to promote new authors, playwrights, and aspiring actors and actresses, and to promote the movie industry, free movies were held in the street. Clark Gable stared with the Blonde Bombshell, Jean Harlow.

Fred Astaire and Ginger Rogers danced their way to fame, as other stars like William Powell, Alice Faye, Kay Francis and Paul Muni made appearances on the big screen. Hancel amusingly speculated how much business we could have drummed up by selling popcorn if the free shows had only occurred a few years earlier.

As Willie and Joseph became involved in basketball practice, the chore of delivering papers fell more often to me. Since we discussed current events in Civic class, I paid more attention to the headlines like: Amelia Earhart, first woman to fly the Atlantic Ocean alone.

Prohibition was repealed. Three point two percent alcoholic beverages became legal. Speak-easies and roadhouses, that once operated secretly, were replaced by dance halls and beer gardens. Swinging and swaying couples glided over glassy floors as the music went round and round. They two-stepped to the music of the big bands making a name for themselves over the airwaves. Dance marathons became the latest fad. Eager couples, aspiring to the fame of Fred Astaire and Ginger Rogers, dragged sleepy-eyed, exhausted partners over polished floors hoping to collect the prize for remaining on their feet the longest. Winning the coveted prize might mean a ticket to Hollywood, to fame and fortune.

Crowds flocked to the Century of Progress Exposition in Chicago. Sally Rand shimmied her way to fame with rhythmic twist of her torso while wagging an ostrich feather fan. Gypsy Rose Lee's talents demonstrated she was more suited as a contortionist than reading tealeaves. Both Big Hancel and Little Hancel attended the fair with a friend. Their round trip train ticket cost three dollars and seventy-five cents. The entire family, except me, went to the Expo. I missed the show of the century.

My current beau was a young man from a neighboring town. We had met while attending a church sponsored summer camp called Quaker Haven. He often drove over to pick me up to attend Sunday services with his family and to spend the day visiting at their home. His parents invited me to accompany the whole family to the fair. His mother and I would share a hotel room, and the father and two sons would share another. His mother wrote a letter to Hancel asking permission for me to accompany them, and explained the arrangements. Hancel would not allow it, saying, "Absolutely not! No daughter of mine is going traipsing off to Chicago with a boy no matter how well she's chaperoned. No! I don't even know those people, and I won't hear another word about it!"

No amount of begging or wheedling could persuade her otherwise. A note declining the invitation stated I should not travel because of my recent appendectomy. She omitted the fact that she thought it an impropriety. Such were the principals and attitudes in those days, strict supervision, instilling morals, and protecting our virginity. - And woe was our trepidation if we disobeyed!

HANCEL'S OLD BEAU REAPPEARS

It was a Friday night. I was awaiting a friend's arrival to pick me up to attend a basketball game. When a knock sounded on the door I assumed it was my friend. I flipped on the porch light and found a stranger standing there. He asked for Hancel. Not knowing his identity, I ask him to wait until I notified her. When she opened the door Hancel's voice, filled with surprise, drifted back to me. I peeked out to see them embracing. Returning to the room, Hancel introduced the handsome gentleman as David, saying that he had once been a very special beau. Taking her hand David said, "Yes. When we were very young Hancel and I planned that someday we would get married. That was before your father appeared on the scene."

My friend's arrival hastened my departure. Since one of my brothers was playing in the game, the rest of the family had already gone. Hancel and David were left alone.

David's wife was dead. They had no children and his life was lonely. He was in town visiting an ailing uncle and had seized the opportunity to renew their friendship. They spent several evenings, and a good portion of their days together reminiscing about old times.

Soon David returned to his home in Ohio. At first his repeat visits occurred regularly. With the passage of time, they became less frequent and were gradually replaced by letter. In time they, too, dwindled. Because of Hancel's responsibilities to her children, she would not consider her own desires until they were all raised. David once again faded from her life. And time marched on.

Family entertainment centered on the radio. The Amos and Andy show was probably the most popular one in those days. At least it was our favorite. Their adventures in operating the Fresh Air Taxi Cab Company amused the masses. If they met with a snag they buzzed Miss Blue to solve the problem. The Kingfish, Beulah, and Madam Queen added zest to the episodes.

Dillinger's crime spree, and reckless violations of the law by petty criminals like Pretty Boy Floyd, kept even our town marshal busy. When the local bank was held up rumors quickly spread that Dillinger's gang was responsible. The town marshal, a friend and neighbor, was shot, and although he was permanently crippled, he escaped with his life. In the neighboring city of Peru, gangsters posing as news reporters armed themselves by robbing the police arsenal. Guilty or not, the crime was blamed on Dillinger. He was eventually captured and confined to the Crown Point jail. His capture and later escape, led to a rash of gangster movies staring Edward G. Robinson and Jimmy Cagney. Although Cagney portrayed tough guys and gangsters, with talent, he later redeemed his persona by being a Yankee Doodle Dandy. He wormed his way into the hearts of his public with dance and song.

Baseball, the sport of the day filtered over the airways. Louis was an avid fan. He was sad when Babe Ruth, the King of Swat, bid farewell and laid down his bat.

FDR's rural electrification program brought electric lights into many homes that were still being illuminated by kerosene lamps, gaslights, and even candles. His other unique ideas "got the country on the move." But in other parts of the world things were moving in the wrong direction. In Germany, the Nazi party selected the swastika as their official symbol. All political parties except the Nazi party was outlawed as a one-time paperhanger, named Adolf Hitler held an entire nation spellbound. Mussolini, who had gradually taken control of Italy, led his army into Ethiopia. Flames of war smoldered as goose-stepping armies rattles their sabers and marched to a dictator's beat.

These events, far away, were less important to me than those in my own life; like attending a De Molay dance. Although I worried that my gown wasn't as fancy as some, my escort assured me that I was the prettiest girl on the dance floor. That was heady stuff! The dance was held at the Masonic Temple in Indianapolis. I was overwhelmed by the enormity and beauty of the ballroom; fascinated by the giant chandelier; the glitz and glitter and mystifying symbols. I felt insignificant in the crowd of snobbish strangers. My escort of the evening was a band member from another school. Although he was a nice young man, I declined any further dates with him. I was more in tune with the home crowd where there was more camaraderie. I wasn't even called Dago anymore, or if I were it was in jest not as an ethic slur.

PROM NIGHT

It was 1935. The Nuremberg laws deprived German Jews of their citizenship. The swastika was exhibited over government buildings throughout Germany and Nazi storm trooper marched though the land. It was the year I graduated from high school.

We didn't have a prom but the junior glass honored the seniors by holding a banquet. Boys didn't rent tuxedoes, as they do today, and girls didn't wear formal gowns. I did, however make a new pink organdy, ankle length, dress for the occasion. The gala was held in the school assemble hall. Food was prepared in the Home Economics classroom by sophomore and freshmen girls, supervised by the teachers, and a group of mothers. This enabled the students to learn the fine points of table etiquette, placing silverware and goblets in their proper place. It gave them a chance to practice their culinary skills, as well as participate in our big event.

No band played, and there was no dancing until the wee hours of the morning. No one drove to neighboring towns for a mid-night dinner, or breakfast the next morning. A lack of moneys made it difficult even to scrape together enough for the affair we did have. Our dates did not buy us corsages. And we did not expect them. We took pleasure in the simple things we had and did not question the lack of that we had never known.

As I mention having no flowers I am reminded of a story about another high school prom in another city. It was during the depression, in 1937, after I married my husband, Ned.

His cousin, Ray, was attending a high school dance in Logansport, Indiana. When a lovely blond girl entered the room, her beauty immediately smote Ray. He could hardly take his eyes off her. And he finally asked her for a dance. They danced dance after dance. During a break, when Ray rejoined his buddies, he announced, "I've just met the girl I'm going to marry" His friends laughed in amusement. But the couple became a twosome.

Prom night was approaching. Ray invited the girl to attend the shin-dig with him. His cousin would also be going and taking a girl. It was the custom, and as such expected, that the boys present their dates with a corsage. One boy's mother was a widow, barely able to support her family. The other family was not much better off since the depression was still creating havoc. There would be no money to buy a corsage. The mothers did not want to put a crimp in the boy's plans but, sooner or later, they would have to realize that there were no funds for flowers. The mothers delayed and procrastinated hoping for a miracle.

The day before the prom, a neighbor and friend was buried. As Ray's mother attended the funeral and watched her friend being laid to rest, surrounded by all the beautiful flowers left in tribute, the answer to her prays lay plainly before her. Maggie would want to share those lovely flowers with the boys. She would be the first to say, "Alice, help yourself to my roses. Make a corsage for Raymond to take to his sweetheart. No one will know where they came from. Sure and it's better for the lad to have them than for them to lay and wither in the sun."

After the crowd dispersed, Alice returned to the cemetery. She selected enough roses and sprigs of fern to make two corsages. She obtained two pearl studded pins and some green tissue paper from a florist friend. She crafted two corsages and twined the stems with scraps of green velveteen. She attached a ribbon to each corsage, wrapped each in the tissue paper and delivered one to the other mother just minutes before the boys arrived home from school. - Such was a mother's love, and such were hard times during the depression.

Ray married the girl before he marched off to fight in the Pacific during World War Two. The cousin fought with the Fourth Marine Division in all its major battles. However, injuries, sustained just prior to their marching into Tokyo prevented him from accompanying them on that historic day.

Years later, when the secret of the prom corsage was revealed, the little blond reveled in the tale more than anyone.

JULIA V. DAWSON

WEDDING BELLS AND WAR DRUMS

After graduating from high school I spent several weeks in Logansport, Indiana, visiting with Grandma Sadie and Aunt Dorothy, Hancel's young unmarried sister. One night Dorothy's escort brought a friend, Ned, along as a blind date for me. When I returned home, Ned drove sixty-five miles every week to court me - when he had the money for gasoline. Although the price of gas was twelve gallons for a dollar, he didn't always have the money. He earned twelve dollars a week working as a shipping clerk in a garment factory.

The only employment available to me, in our small town, was as a hired girl minding children and helping with housework for the family that owned and operated the canning factory. I also worked in the canning factory during tomato and sweet corn season. I enrolled in postgraduate courses in Latin and Literature at the local high school conducted by student teacher from Taylor University. In 1936 I succumbed to the language of love. I put away The Lady Of The Lake to become the lady of the house. Ned and I were married.

Hancel was not happy to see me leave. In retrospect I should have remained at home longer to help her. But I was ardently wooed with irresistible whispers of an idyllic life in a cottage built for two "East Of The Sun And West Of The Moon." In more realistic moments the whispered word were "I Can't Give You Anything But Love, Baby."

Ned went to work for U.S. Steel, and we moved to Gary, Indiana. The average pay was two dollars and seventy-six cents per day, for an eight-hour day. As a steel worker Ned's pay was three dollars and seventy-six cents a day. Prosperity was still around the corner, but things were looking up. The idyllic cottage for two became two furnished light-house-keeping - rooms; a living room bedroom combination that rented for seven dollars and fifty cent a week. The only memorable feature was the window box used as a refrigerator. At home we used a wooden icebox. A door opened on the top and allowed ice to be dropped in. A pan always sat under the cabinet to catch the water that dripped as the ice melted. Ice was purchased only on weekends. A card, placed in the window, directed the iceman as to the size to be delivered; a twenty-five, fifty or hundred pound chunk. Ice was packed on the floor of a truck and covered with a canvas tarp. After being chipped into the designated size, it was carried into the house with tongs. As a kid following the ice truck on a hot day was great fun. The friendly iceman was always willing to chip off slivers of ice to hand out to kids that tagged behind the truck. In 1938 we bought our first electric refrigerator, a Sears Roebuck Coldspot.

Reminiscing about the ice card in the window reminds me of another card often nailed to the front of a house, as we were growing up. A red quarantine card notified the public when someone in the household was ill with a contagious disease. It's presence confined entire households, for weeks. It listed the malady; measles, scarlet fever, or whatever. A hapless child unlucky enough to have been quarantined was shunned for days after being released, for fear of spreading the disease. No one was allowed to enter or depart during the quarantine period. Trespasser could be fined two hundred dollars, jailed, or both.

Even before we bought the refrigerator, the first piece of furniture purchased was a console radio. It was delivered the same day that the Prince of Wales announced, in his famous abdication speech, that he was renouncing the throne of England "in order to marry the woman I love."

Joseph was already married, Willie was the next to do so. Only Hancel's two youngest children remained at home. They continued delivering the newspapers.

The country emerged gradually from the depression. Ned's regular paycheck allowed us a few luxuries, such as attending a circus. I had never been to a circus. Another couple accompanied us to Hammond. After the performance we drove to Chicago to see the city. We topped the evening off by dining at Sun Lee's Chinese Restaurant on 22nd. Street. For fifty cents we were served a nine course meal; soup, choice of entrees, dessert, green tea and fortune cookies. My old menu, yellow with age reads: Try our 9 courses. Chinese Dinner, Liberal Portions, Deliciously Prepared. Beef Rice — with mushrooms, water chestnuts, poached eggs. The souvenir menu shows how low prices were in those days. But fifty cents was as hard to come by then as twenty dollars is today.

The days passed quickly. Hancel's letters kept me informed of my brothers and sister. Louis played in the high school basketball tournament, going to the state. Although their team lost, Louise was awarded the Most Valuable Player Of the Year trophy. He still remains an avid sports fan. —Incidentally, the nickname, Bounce, attached to him years ago, still identifies him even today.

Shirley Temple was captivating the hearts of moviegoers. A little known actor by the name of Ronald Reagan was making his first movie, and Frank Sinatra appeared on the Major Bowes amateur hour. Bennie Goodman's and Harry James's music filtered the airwaves, and Gene Krupa 's toe tapping' cadence set couples swinging as he "beat it. Daddy, eight to the bar." The dirigible, Hindenburg, exploded in mid air, and Amelia Earhart disappeared on a flight over the Pacific Ocean.

To us, the most important event of the year was the birth of our first son. Although that was not earth shaking news, events elsewhere set entire continents trembling. Italy withdrew from the League of Nations. Hitler's goose-stepping troops stormed into Austria and annexed it. In China, Japan invaded Manchuria. General Franco defeated the Loyalist troops in Spain. Neville Chamberlain said, "I believe there will be peace in our time." France and England declared war on Germany as Hitler's army invaded Czechoslovakia and Poland.

In the United States, Orson Wells dismayed the population with a radio production of The War Of The Worlds. Many actually believed Martians were invading our planet. As Christmas approached Santa Clause appeared at the Montgomery Ward stores and passed out a free comic book, which introduced Rudolph, the Red-nosed Reindeer. A few years later the Ward store where our son obtained his copy, on Broadway, in Gary, Indiana, burned to the ground. That old copy, discarded long ago, would be worth mega buck today.

Fires also burned throughout Europe as the war escalated to Denmark. Hitler declared the purpose of that invasion was to assure that country's neutrality. His troops invaded Belgium, Holland, and Luxemburg. France felt secure behind the Maginot Line but, with the German army's attack, the defenses collapsed and German troops marched into France. Italy declared war on France, and in England Winston Churchill promised "only blood, sweat, and tears." The US vowed to stay out of Europe's war but when German U-boats attacks drew closer to US shores, it became harder for America to avoid the conflict. - And Kate Smith sang God Bless America. The war spread to Russia. The sub-zero weather killed friend and foe alike as men froze in their saddles.

In 1940 seventy-five thousand men were drafted in the first peacetime draft. With production of armaments, steel mills rolled at full capacity. Everyone was working again. German air power exceeded England's five to one, so plane production increased. K rations were manufactured, along with blackout-lamps, sub-machine guns and cartridge cases. Ordnance plants ran at full capacity as the US became the Arsenal of Democracy by sending aid to their allies. America could no longer stay out of the war. The Civil Defense mobilized. When Japan attacked Pearl Harbor America was involved in a war on two fronts. Joseph joined the Fighting Sea- bees. Louis was putting himself through Ball State University, in Muncie, by delivering papers,

167

but he quit to enlist in the Navy. Neither son told Hancel of their plans for joining until after enlisting.

As more and more men left to fight in the war, woman joined the work force. Rosie the Riveter worked the swing shift on the production line. Hancel went to work in a glass factory, in Gas city, making medicine bottles, and making more money than she had made in her entire life. If her sons could fight in the war, exposed to danger, she would do her part, too. My sister completed her business course and went to work in the office at the same factory as Hancel.

Working along side of men, women began wearing trousers, pants suits, or slacks. Hancel continued wearing her usual starched, button-down-the-front percale print dresses. Sophisticated ladies sheathed their legs in the new, hard to get nylon stockings, when available. When they were not, they smeared colored goo on their legs to give the appearance of hosiery. The absence of a full fashion seam down the middle of the leg was a dead give away that they were fake.

THE WAR YEARS

With hoards of men in the armed forces to feed and clothe, rationing began at home; sugar, oils, butter, and meats. Shoes were limited and cloth was sewn into uniforms. A long queued up line at a grocery store was an indication that an item in short supply was being sold, bacon, cigarettes, or nylons. Gasoline and tires were rationed. Due to tire and gas rationing we were unable to visit our respective families for what seemed an eternity. After hoarding gasoline coupons for months we finally made the trip. Returning home we were forced to repair three flat tires. We drove the last lap on two rims. The next morning a neighbor complained of a sleepless night after some poor SOB awakened her clattering by her house on their rims. I admitted we were the culprits. The car was parked in the side yard, and jacked up until tires became available, after the war.

Since he worked in an essential war industry, Ned was deferred in the draft. He received numerous awards, approved by the War Production Drive Committee of Carnegie Steel Corp. He also designed and patented an Extensometer, which accelerated production by seventy-five hours when put to use in the mill. He contributed to the war effort even though he did not don a uniform and march to the beat of a drum.

We lived in the small community of Lake Station. It's only claim to fame was that Abraham Lincoln once slept at the old Lake Tavern Inn that once served as a stagecoach stop on the old Chicago Road. Due to the town's proximity to the steel mills, a vital war production area, the Civil Defense required all residents to have their blood types tattooed on their body.

Since it was patriotic to conserve food for the fighting men, the government advocated that everyone should plant a garden, a Victory Garden. We rented a plot of ground, sowed seeds and sat back and waited for nature to make them grow. With the car parked for the duration, we rowed our boat across Deep River to cultivate the patch. As the plants began to grow, rabbits nibbled on the tender young shoots. Bean beetles and grasshoppers attacked in droves. But we produced, and harvested, succulent vegetables for the table. I'm not sure how much we helped the war effort, but it offered us pleasure and supplied us with tender ears of sweet corn.

Due to the meat shortage we decided to raise chickens. Why, I'll never fathom since Ned wouldn't eat chicken. But he built a chicken shed and fenced in a pen. We bought twenty-five baby chicks that grew and mature into drumsticks, wishbones, and soup stock. When they were fryer size, Ned absolutely refused to kill them. A neighbor graciously performed the deed for me. Until, finally, his cousin, mentioned in the corsage tale was visiting us, while at home on leave before shipping out, and was persuaded to execute the remaining flock, in lieu of purchasing more chicken feed. Having already invested enough to consider the experiment a financial loss, I spent more money and bought canning jars. I plucked the birds, packed them in jars, processed them, and set them in picture perfect row on the root cellar shelves.

For some long forgotten special occasion I wanted a navy blue blouse. None was available so I dyed a white one in the largest vessel I owned, my big soup pot. After completing the task I scoured and cleaned the pan. A few days later, I decided to make chicken gumbo soup. I opened a jar of chicken, put it in the stewpot and on the stove to cook. When it was briskly boiling I opened the lid to add vegetables. The broth and the meat was a beautiful pea green. Although the residue of the dye had not been apparent to the naked eye, the solution had permeated the pours of the pot. The blue of the dye blended with the yellow of the chicken fat to create a shade of green that could never be duplicated on an artist's palette! —So much for our part in the war effort.

Scrap drives were held. Discarded junk was collected and turned into war implements. Old plowshares were beaten into tanks. Posters asked, "What can you spare that they can wear?" Clothing was collected and shipped over seas for destitute refugees. Newspapers pictured GI Joe tacking up signs that read Kilroy Was Here. We all wondered who Kilroy was. Another sad news item announced that U.S. Army Private Eddie Slovak was executed, before a firing squad. It was the first such execution since the Civil War.

Hancel walked to the post office daily hoping for a letter from one of her sons. The new vee-mail allowed planes to carry more mail. One day, as she walked by the house of the man who had taken the player piano in trade on the farm, his widow, familiar with the tale, called to her. She was going to sell the old piano and wondered if Hancel might want to buy it back before she advertised it for sale.

Being sentimental, Hancel bought it. What a surprise I had on my next visit to spy the old piano sitting in the parlor. Lined in a row atop it were the high school graduation pictures of her five children. Through the following years as my children, and my nieces and nephews, visited their grandmother they pumped and peddled out old familiar tunes. Hancel once offered the piano to me, but I had no way to transport it to northern Indiana. In hindsight, I wish I had somehow found a way.

Louie wrote, "My ship was anchored in a port in Okinawa. When I learned Joseph's unit was nearby I sought, and received, permission to travel to their base. Locating his tent, I found Joe sitting at a desk with his back to the open tent flap. I silently entered and placed my hand on my brother's shoulder. You can imagine his surprise when he turned and saw me standing there.

Joe had gathered huge mahogany logs and planks that littered the island. During idle moments, and with but a few wood-working tools at his disposal, he transformed the beautiful timbers into a desk and the seat upon which he sat."

For years, Hancel saved every letter her sons had written to her. Somehow, through the ensuing years, the old letters vanished. Today they would disclose many interesting, and historical, facts about the war. Like the two that I will record below. One appeared on the front page of our hometown paper as news from a local service boy.

Leyte, Nov. 20/1944
(Delayed -passed censor)

Dear Mom:

My ship was anchored in Leyte Bay. One afternoon a PT boat tied up astern of it. We were lucky enough to have obtained a movie to be shown that evening. The boys from the PT boat came over to attend the movie. Imagine my surprise when I heard my name called by a familiar voice. I turned to discover my old buddy and schoolmate, J.R.

After the show J.R. stayed aboard and stood watch with me until midnight. During those hours we talked about everything and everybody, catching up on news from home. J.R. invited me to accompany him the next day on patrol. I was ready and waiting when the PT boat arrived twenty minutes early. An officer from our ship also went along.

With other ships surrounding us, we steamed along at full speed for a trip of one hundred and seventy-five miles. Our destination was Ormoc Bay on the other side of Leyte Island. The Japs still hold Ormoc. We had air cover until dark. Then it was each PT boat on its own, ready for anything.

For hours nothing happened. Suddenly, as we neared Ormoc Bay, we began to sight Jap barges about a half-mile off shore. J.R.'s boat had taken the lead since the lead boat had suffered a minor casualty. The guns from J.R.'s boat poured out shells as we made a run for the barges, concentrating on one barge. The guns hit that Jap barge so often it broke in half and sank. Other boats also found their targets. All totaled, we sank four barges.

As we turned away, full speed ahead, the Japs returned fire. Bullets whined overhead. Troops on shore were also directing rifle fire at us.

We circled the bay for an hour and a half. We came within five hundred yards of the docks before we spotted two Jap luggers and pursued them. When we finally caught up to them, we were between two small islands in a pass barely two miles wide. With guns blazing we made a run for them. I was manning a twin-mounted machine gun on the starboard side. Our boats made another circle, attacking. We sank a lugger. After sinking the first lugger, we proceeded toward the remaining one. We made three runs before sinking it. We were under attack all the time. One of our ships was hit by fire, or by a bomb.

After the battle, our boats converged in the middle of the pass to take care of the wounded. One man had been killed, three seriously injured, and others suffered minor injuries.

After taking five of the injured men aboard we began making our way out of the channel.

On our return trip the boat that had been hit had two engines fail. We came along side and took aboard the three critically injured men and sped toward an army post. We reached the post a few minutes before dawn. We obtained blood plasma, picked up an army corpsman, and headed for a destroyer that was patrolling the area. We transferred the casualties aboard the destroyer.

The cook, on the destroyer, gave us a big pot of steaming hot coffee. I consumed three cups. Coffee never tasted so good. It had been raining constantly since about midnight and we were drenched to the bone. We went below, where it was dry, and made ourselves comfortable. We fell asleep immediately. The boat returned to Leyte.

I've run into J.R. three times since. Each time after he has been out raiding. He casually says. 'It's all in the days work.' He tells of troops laden barges sunk, a transport or beach patrol craft torpedoed, or of strafing Jap positions on the beach. Action packed attacks that mete destruction to the enemy. The men aboard those PT boats deserve praise for the nasty job well done. By comparison my life is much more secure. I am safe and well. Do not worry about me.

> Your loving son, Louis
> Signalman first class
> U.S. Navy

My sister's beau enlisted in the Merchant Marines. He was stationed in New Orleans while attending officers training. School. He purposed by letter, and asked her to join him there so they could get married before he shipped out. She accepted. Hancel accompanied her daughter to see her safely wed. The couple had a week together before his ship sailed.

Our youngest son was born in December 1945. Sis took a leave of absence and came to help me with our other two children. When she walked in the door, I couldn't believe the beautiful young lady was my little sister, grown up and married. Hancel arrived later, by bus, to spend the Christmas holidays with us. After the long separation, what a holiday that was!

The rest is history and bears no repeating. With the death of FDR, Harry Truman became the president of the United States. In order to end the war in the Pacific, and to save many service boys' lives, the atomic bomb was dropped on Japan. The following letter is the last one I received from Louis before he returned home.

First Ship in Tokyo Bay at End of War

Tokyo Bay, Japan
Sept. 6/1945

Dear Sis and family:

Greetings to all from Tokyo, a city, which normally has a population of 7,000,000 people but scarcely, has 2,000,000 now. They have all quit the city thinking harm would come to them.

We came in a little after nine o'clock this morning, piloted down the channel by a Jap civilian. He really thought he was important. We are the first ship in here, the inner harbor of Tokyo Bay.

We arrived at Yokahama, about twenty miles away, the day before the final surrendering ceremonies, for which we had a ringside seat. A few days before that, we had witnessed the surrendering of the Yokahama (sp) Naval Base. The Jap Vice Admiral really got all shook up about it.

The army is supposed to have moved into Tokyo today at nine o'clock. I guess they did but haven't seen any troops as yet.

You are no doubt surprised to receive a letter with this news in it. Censoring has ceased as of a few days ago.

I am writing this letter while on watch. There are no ships within fifteen or twenty miles of us, so there is no signaling to do. I have to keep the lights going just in case a crazy Jap happens around. I have a Thompson machine gun with me, and there's a sentry down on the dock with another. Three or four stand guard down on the pier, which has warehouses all up and down it. We have nothing to worry about but we are ready just in case. Those I have seen on the docks, today, are scared stiff of us. I had better get out and take a look around. Hope you can read this as I have rushed through it.

Don't know when I'll get home. Rotation will be up in two months.

So Long, Much Love, Louis

When Louis's ship was anchored in the Philippines, near Leyte, a patrol including Louis debarked and went ashore. They waded through debris and mire to arrive at a small village. Louis told the following tale of that experience: "At first the villagers secreted themselves in their homes. Upon discovering that the troops were Americans, they sent a young man out to act as interpreter. They opened their doors and beckoned to us to come inside. They offered to feed us and to launder our mud covered garments.

As we made ready to depart they invited us to return the next day for a pig roast. Since it was uncertain how long the ship would remain anchored in the bay, we declined. We promised to return if the ship did not sail, and if we were granted permission to do so."

Before leaving the village, Louis and the young interpreter agreed to write to each other. They become pen pals. Through them Hancel and the guide's sister began to correspond with each other. In exchange for Hancel sending her items impossible to buy in the islands because of the war, soap, toothpaste etc., Hancel received lovely gifts of embroidered linens, pieces of pure silk, and crafted seashell articles. The two continued writing for several years. I still have some of those gifts.

After the war Hancel continued to work in the glass factory. Although she worked along side of men, performing the exact work as men, bore the same blisters and back aches, she never received equal pay. Woman's Lib was a concept still undreamed of. The situation was accepted without protest.

For years she suffered with ulcerated varicose veins on her ankles. No matter what treatment was administered they always remained swollen and sore. They would drain, heal, and burst open again.

At the completion of twenty-five years of employment, an item appeared in the factory paper. It bore the heading "Interesting People" It related Hancel's story of how she raised

177

her five children, alone. The article again stated that many people often wondered how she ever did it during the trying times of the depression. It added, "A lesser person would have taken an easier way out." But she did, and we all led successful lives.

After the war Joseph returned to his job at the Johnson Glass factory in Hartford City, where he had been employed almost from the day he graduated from high School. He gradually advanced to become Superintendent of the plant. He raised two sons and two daughters.

Using his many talents, he built a home on the property that was once the little farmland. An interesting thing was that, through the ensuing years, a small lake gradually developed along the farm boundary lines. As children our favorite play area was a site under a large elm tree, an area of sandy soil where a spring flowed. We often found Indian arrowheads buried in the sand. Sometimes the spring flowed, but often it remained dormant for long stretches at a time. Finally it disappeared completely after a new culvert was constructed under the railroad tracks. Perhaps the spring was blocked and began flowing in a new location, and through the years created the new lake.

Willie worked for a utility company in Muncie, Indiana. Since he and his wife, Norma, had two children, and because his employment was considered a vital industry, he was exempt from the draft. He was a good husband and father, and a good citizen. He led a successful life.

When Louis returned from the war he attended Purdue University before accepting a job for the American Fruit Company. For eighteen months he worked as an accountant on a banana plantation in Panama. Returning to the states, he worked for a time at a Warner Gear factory in Muncie. After he married he built a house, next door to Hancel on the property that had once revert back to the county for taxes owed; the site where the Green family once lived. Later he became sales representative for a light bulb company. Through contacts with a storeowner he acquired a rural grocery store in Mt. Zion.

Mt Zion was one of the little villages that sprang up with the discovery of natural gas. Established in 1895, it was named for a church located in the area. During the boom period the store building housed a pharmacy and grocery store on the first floor. An outside stairway led to a huge community hall, or lodge meeting place. The room resembled a dance hall with a raised stage at the front of the room, and was the center of attraction for many performances. Also on the second floor, across from the hall were a series of sleeping rooms. In the early days the village consisted of two other grocery stores, a hardware store, barbershop, and other establishments. When the natural gas dwindled, drills became silent, oil people moved to new fields, and the community became a ghost town. Even today, a few derricks are still pumping in the nearby area.

When Louis and Joan, his wife, took over the store, sometime in the fifties, there was a steady flow of customers, farmers from the surrounding area. As supermarkets, and shopping malls were constructed in nearby cities, business slumped. Louis became a factory representative for Indiana Glass, selling glass items to florist and gift shops. Doors that opened into their living quarters allowed Joan to operated the store along with tending to their daughter and five sons.

After the war, Sis's husband worked for the Veterans Administration, starting at the hospital in Marion, Indiana. Through the years he transferred to various hospitals in many states. As Fiscal Officer, each move was a promotion. After being transferred to the Bay Pines Hospital in Clearwater, Florida their four children voted down another move. Sis worked for several years in an office for Eckerd Drugs. Once, while visiting them I noticed a lovely painting on an artist's easel. I asked who painted the picture. She said her children, all attending college at the time, were all so smart and talented that she had to do something to improve herself, so she enrolled in art classes. The painting attested to her talent.

As a mother of three, when faced with the empty nest syndrome, I worked for eighteen years as a licensed real estate saleslady in Lake and Porter Counties during the era that the Port Of Indiana, and the new town of Portage were being developed. — All our success is attributed to the exemplary influence Hancel bestowed in our lives.

Hancel in Florida

SADIE BREAKS HER HIP

When her youngest daughter, Dorothy, married and left home, Sadie continued working. The families for whom she worked looked upon her as a loving Aunty, and considered her an extended part of their families. She earned enough for her simple need, and a few pleasures, and in so doing savored her independence. Unfortunately, after a few years, she fell and broke her hip. She could no longer support herself, nor maintain her modest apartment. Her children arranged to divide her time in their home. By each sharing in her custodial care, it offered a periodic break to all. It also allowed Sadie a change of scenery and life was more interesting for her.

Hancel was still working at the glass factory. When it was her time to keep Sadie, they had little time together. Hancel had been alone for so long she had become set in her ways. Her routine consisted of going to work, cleaning house, preparing meals, going to church, walking to the post office in hopes of receiving a letter from one of her children. Louis and Joseph both lived nearby. She found it hard to adjust to another's presence. Two lonely ladies who could have enjoyed each others company did not seem to accommodate each other. The days were lonesome for Sadie. When it was time for her to stay with Hancel, Joseph and I developed the habit of having her visit with us. My children loved her. She entertained them by reciting stories of the olden days; of political rallies held around bonfires while singing songs and listening to speeches.

One autumn when Joseph brought Sadie to our home for her yearly visit, we walked outside to enjoy the lovely night. It was October and acorns littered the ground. Since she walked with a cane, we were concerned that Sadie would step on one of the fallen pellets and lose her footing. After she was seated, as we sat enjoying the night noises, the stars, and each other's company, Joseph looked up at the sky and asked Sadie if she had heard about Sputnik. Pointing to a tiny glowing object gliding through the sky, he told her it was a satellite sailing through space; it belonged to Russia, and was called Sputnik. He added that Russia had beaten America in the space race by putting the first satellite in orbit. He said that the United States was working on rockets, satellites, and space ships that would soar above the Universe, and soon astronauts would circle the globe. The U.S. was working on something called the Vanguard missile, and "Some day, perhaps during your life time, Man will transcend earth to land on the moon."

Sadie could not understand such things. Born during the age of the horse and buggy, she had witnessed the creation of the railroads, with steam engines that belched smoke and cinders. She lived during the era of the horseless carriage when drivers wore goggles and long duster coats. She had seen the development of electric lights, telephone, the automobile, airplane, and the radio. She was thrilled, but apprehensive, when traveling by plane. But a space ship that would carry men to the moon was more than she could comprehend. She hoped to live long enough to witness it, at least to be able to watch it on the newfangled television.

Joseph reminded her that President Truman had delivered his first live coast-to-coast television speech in 1951. "Since then more and more people now own T. V. sets. It's the source of minute- by- minute news programs, and there's no doubt that, when Man lands on the moon, it will be televised."

If I passed Sadie, while doing my household chores, she would reach out with her cane and catch me by my ankle. Then, pulling a deck of card from her pocket she would say, "Kiddo, it's time for a break. Let's have a quick game of hearts." We all loved her. - That's not to say that Hancel did not love her. But life left little time for Hancel to love, only to labor.

THE SPACE AGE

Hancel was never one to complain or to give in to aches and pains. Year ago, when she developed a toothache she suffered in silence until the pain was unbearable. The dentist had deserted the town a few years after the glass factory closed. With no transportation to one in another city, her only recourse was to go to the local medical doctor. (Dr. Zimmer was dead) With no anesthesia to ease her pain several teeth were extracted. She continued on her paper route and performed her daily chores.

Knowing she did not coddle herself, when she wrote of having problems with her gall bladder, I knew it was serious. She had retired and was drawing Social Security benefits, and now had time to scheduled surgery.

I went to the hospital to be with her. For forty-eight hours I stayed in her room, curled up in a chair. With each passing minute I feared for her life. A tube inserted through her throat to drain away green bile caused her excruciating pain and discomfort. She hardly knew that I was there; such was her suffering.

Joseph appeared for a visit on the second evening. When she spied him her face beamed with joy. She reached for his hand and whispered, "Oh, Joe." At that moment, I realized how much she had depended upon him through the years, confiding in him, and saddling him with problems she could not discuss with her younger children. He was there for her during all those hard times and lonely years.

As she improved, I read the papers to her. How the Russian cosmonaut, Yuri Gagarian, had just completed a flight in space. He described the feeling of weightlessness as he hurtled through the boundless expanse, at a speed of 17,000 miles per hour. He said it was eerie to watch objects floating around him, weightless in space. He described the earth as a beautiful blue globe. He could not see the moon but the stars were visible and the sun was ten times brighter than when seen from earth. He described his flight as he traveled over continents, islands, rivers, and larger bodies of water.

The Space age had arrived. The Russian Premier, Nikita Khrushchev, bragged that America should "Try to catch us if you can." It looked like Russia was winning the war race.

As I read these articles, I said to her, "Mom, just think, someday you may fly to the moon. Can you imagine that?"

"I still find it hard to comprehend airplanes, filled with passengers, lifting into the air much less trying to imagine a flight to the moon. I'm sure I'll never see it but maybe one of my children will."

Although flight in space had been achieved, a more familiar mode of travel was in trouble. The railroads were going bankrupt. Many companies sought aid, or subsidies, from the federal and state governments to keep their trains operating. Others abandoned lines, curtailed services, or discontinued it.

The Iron Horse was in trouble. Workmen, who, for years, even during the lean years of the depression, felt secure in their railroad jobs, were finding themselves laid off, or let go. The hue and cries of the populace were: "Save the railroads. Forget the Space program. It's a waste of tax payers money." The new was denounced, and censured, in favor of the old and familiar.

But more searching minds said, "The program should, and must continue at any cost. It is essential that America catches up with, and even surpass Russian in the exploration of space. It is a matter of national security."

HANCEL'S WEDDING

Hancel's retirement years were filled with the antics of two little granddaughters. Joseph was raising a second family. Since he and his wife both worked, Hancel took care of the girls. She looked forward to their daily arrival. When they entered school, she was again left with a void in her life.

An old gentleman moved in next door to her. Greetings, spoken in passing, gradually developed into tid-bits of news and gossip exchanged over the back yard fence; comments about the weather, current events, family information and details of their respective lives. As their friendship grew Hancel sent him toothsome treats, a wedge of pie, a slice of cake, or goodies that a man would not prepare for himself. They began going on shopping excursions, to a movies, or for Sunday drives.

One day as I visited, Hancel asked what I thought about them getting married. I was stunned! But it was her decision. Concealing my feelings, I answered. "If you think you can find happiness, go for it."

The telephone buzzed with conversation between her children. As a daughter my first inclination was WHY? Why, after all the years that had passed, should she wed again? But realizing how lonely her life had been, and still must be for her. I reasoned why shouldn't she grab for the brass ring? Why not enjoy her golden years with a companion?

Her sons felt differently. Louis thought it ridiculous. Willie didn't want her to marry, and Joseph wouldn't even discuss it. Hancel knew nothing of the talk that went on behind her back! Soon a wedding date was set. At seventy-three years of age, after being a widow for a half century, Hancel got married.

Her children were all present. We tried to make it a gala affair; with flowers, a wedding cake and punch. When the minister asked, "Who gives this woman to be wed?" Between blowing his nose and wiping his eyes, Joseph answered, "I do."

Willie left the room, momentarily, to hide his flow of tears. Louis cried, unabashedly. Sis quickly busied herself at the bunch bowl, and, although the tears did not show, I silently wept for all the long lonely years Hancel had endured.

Like a couple of lovebirds they moved into a home. When spring arrived they planted tulip bulbs and hyacinths, and a vegetable garden. They were happy doing things together. — But it was like the calm before a storm.

Willie was the first to notice. On a visit he found Hancel confined to her bedroom. Her husband said she shut herself in her room quite often of late. She was not acting like her old self. Willie made an appointment for her to see a doctor. He found no physical problems beyond those normal for her age.

But there are things beyond the sound of the stethoscope, beyond an MRI and medical diagnosis. Much is beyond the mysterious probe of the physician. It became apparent that Hancel was in deep depression. She left her room only to prepare meals, which she seldom ate. A day came, while talking to her by telephone, that I knew things were not right in her mind. She rambled about Louie, about James Allan. How he wanted her to marry him but she declined because of her children. She was in such a state of mind that she referred to herself as a woman that would certainly go to hell for having loved others after Louie's death. I convinced her she was mistaken in such thoughts. "I know of no one more virtuous or moral. Certainly you were entitled to companionship and love. Your path will be to heaven, not hell. No one is more deserving."

She wondered why she had married; didn't understand why she had done so. It was then that I realized, even at the time she married, she had been mentally confused.

I suggested that she come visit me for a while, to sort things out, and then she would be ready to return home. I watched her

187

pack unlikely items. At the inclusion of a picture album, I was not concerned. When she removed a large wooden framed picture of Louie from the wall, I suggested she leave it. She was adamant that the picture would go. From habit, and years of deferring to her judgment, I acquiesced.

She asked me to stop at the bank. Upon returning to the car, she informed me that she had signed release papers on her home. The house that had been her and Louie's first home. It was then that I learned, many years ago, in dire need and desperation, she had opted for a life estate in her home in exchange for a small quarterly income.

I pointed out that her life was not over yet, and, and under a life estate, she could still keep her home. She answered, "I was never happy with the situation. From the moment I signed the papers I felt I was accepting charity."

"You should not have thought of it as charity. The church officials, although helping you, were good businessmen. Today the lending institutions would call it a reverse mortgage."

Unfortunately, leaving her home and familiar surroundings, at her age, had done something psychologically to her. Her mind could not cope. I realized she had merely extricated herself from a situation she could no longer tolerate. More lonely years.

I also think, it was at that moment that I knew she would not be returning home. She was placing herself in the position that her children would look after her. After a prolonged stay, when her husband called for her to return, she absolutely refused to return. I would not make her do so.

She finally obtained a divorce, with the name Benedict restore. The marriage had lasted a few months into the second year. Even after the decision was made, the idea of divorce was abhorrent to her.

"Divorce at my age! What will people say? What would my father think if he were alive?"

"Don't think of what people will think. Your family should have got over the shock of divorce years ago when your cousin

Bill married Josie, and later divorced Goldie, Maggie. Pearl, and Marie."

"Yes, but Josie died in childbirth and Bill was always searching for his lost love."

"Maybe the same could be said of you, that you were searching for a love you lost years ago."

She remained depressed. She sat for hours staring into space. Where she had once read the daily papers from cover to cover, she no longer opened the pages. She would not watch television, participate in family conversations, and took no interest in her great-grandchildren. She was utterly confused.

It was while Hancel was in this mental confusion that we received a phone call telling us of Sadie's death. At ninety-four years of age, her life had spanned almost a century. A century that progressed from the horse and buggy to the space age. She didn't witness man's walk on the moon. She did hear the famous words "In the beginning God created the Heavens and Earth" transmitted, via satellite, from Apollo Eight as it circled the moon on the first lunar flight. She watched it on television.

The years that spanned her life had truly been a Century of Progress. Candlepower and gaslights were exchanged for electric lights. The horse and plow moved over for the tractor and combines. Man had produced trains, automobiles, airplanes, and submarines. They perfected radar and sonar. Television ushered in the telecommunication era. With scientific knowledge Man discovered electrons, protons and molecules. He split the atom, discovered penicillin and polo vaccines, and miracle drugs that eradicated smallpox, and other infectious diseases. All were as miraculous in their day as the space ships are today. Her life events, had they been recorded, would have furnish material for a good book.

When Hancel refused to return home, I began putting her affairs in order. I updated insurance policies and legal papers. With five offspring, each with different ideas of how things should be handled, sometimes confusion reigned. Louis assumed her guardianship. He bought a small house next door to his home where she spent her summers. During the winter months she made her home in Florida with her youngest daughter. Under the care of geriatric doctors, and proper medications she improved monthly. She became her old self. Sis kept us informed with letters, like in the following:

"She no longer sits for hours staring into space. It's like she's deep into Transcendental Meditations, thinking good thoughts and not dwelling on the sorrow that pervaded her life. I tell her 'Let your mind float, relax, close your eyes and relive pleasant moments.' I sometimes catch her smiling to herself."

Although we all took our turns for visits, Hancel was happiest living with her youngest daughter. As the last child to leave home they seemed to have more in common. After a days work Sis would do something special with her. They might go shopping, drive along the beach, go to a movie and stop for a treat. She knew just how to please her; how to pamper and placate her.

Little Hancel and Husband

THE KENNEDY SPACE CENTER

In 1972, at the age of fifty-nine, my husband suddenly announced that he was taking early retirement. As a fifty-three year old active real estate sales-lady, I was not ready to confine myself to a rocking chair! In fairness to him I agreed to work part time so we could travel in our recreational vehicle.

Hancel treasured letters. She saved them, sorted them, labeled each with the writer's name, and tied them into bundles. I later retrieved the following one, written after touring the Kennedy Space Center. Since the theme of this tale is from the horse and buggy to the Space Age, it seems appropriate that it be included here.

Feb. 1972
On the Road

Dear Mom:

Our visit to the Kennedy Space Center will probably be the most memorable part of our entire trip. I'll never comprehend the Space program. Tourism here is a mighty big business. For two dollars and fifty cents, each, we toured the complex in a comfortable Greyhound bus. The two hour and fifteen minute tour covered the Mission Control Center, Air Force Space Museum, Air Base, Apollo and Lunar launch pads, and the Industrial Building. That building alone covers nine acres of land and is fifty-two stories high. A huge door reaches to the top.

We saw the mighty muscle machine that moves the missiles and rockets, a section at a time, into the huge building to be assembled. Each section is hoisted by cranes and pulleys and moved, by the muscle machine, onto tracks that carries it to launch pads and different complexes.

Complex is the word for it! I'll never understand it. All I know for sure is that they shot the crew to the moon. This I know because we have watched it on television. They bounced about on the moon picking up Genesis Rocks and lunar dust, as they announce to the World, "We leave as we came, in peace for all Mankind."

Our guide told us, "On the next flight to the moon plans are to take a small electric powered automobile, weighing about four hundred and forty pounds. It will be left there for future astronauts to use. Space stations will be used as shuttle service centers between earth and the moon. Satellites will be used as air traffic control centers, weather prediction stations, natural resource, pollution and environmental studies. Now that will be another giant leap for Mankind, since the first fifteen-minute walk in space.

We missed the Astronauts but while touring the training building, where tests are conducted and flights practices, we did see a pair of Hush Puppy shoes that John Glenn had removed before entering the module. They had been left as a prop to humanize the Astronaut.

Astronauts work for ten hours a day, sometimes for ten months a year. They work under the exact simulated conditions that will be encountered in space on actual flights. It is grueling, exhausting work. They're pioneers, like your ancestors who came to Indiana in a covered wagon. At least they had their feet on solid ground. Until now, I've looked upon these shots as a Flash Gordon; you read it in the comics, kind of deal. Unbelievable! But having seen it, here, I am a convert. The medical knowledge gained is tremendous. Who knows what other wonders may still be discovered as they "sail on the new ocean."

We were allowed to take movies everywhere except in the astronauts training building. We took pictures of the space ship in which John Glenn circled the earth, as well as missiles of every size and shape.

193

There are as many shapes and sizes in the crowd taking the tour. It's entertaining to watch the tourist. In this unisex age it isn't hard to sort the men from the boys, but we have to look twice to distinguish the males from the females. With so many boys with long hair, and girls with hair cut short, I take care when queuing up in line at the golden room.

The area is also a game preserve. The only animal we saw was an armadillo waddling down a path. It's like a beautiful park here, green and groomed; flowers border walkways. Wood, water and wastelands have been put to useful purpose. There are enough missiles to mystify the millions who take these tours. I wouldn't have missed it for a million, this New Frontier exhibit.

Until later, It's Your loving daughter, Julia

A BICENTENNIAL CELEBRATION

In August 1976, we were visiting Hancel in Mt. Zion before her regular fall departure to Florida. Celebrations and programs were being held, state wide, for America's bicentennial, or two hundredth birthday. In Bluffton, Indiana, a few miles away, the attraction was a re-enactment of the Civil War battle of Fredericksburg. Louis, an avid Civil War enthusiast, invited us to attend the ceremony with him.

Participating were artillery units, infantry and cavalry soldiers from Indiana, Illinois, Michigan, and as far away as Tennessee. Men who, as a hobby, had scrupulously studied details of uniforms, battle maneuvers, and events of that day. Wives, clad in period costumes, acted as nurses and camp followers. Young sons added realism through their roles as drummer boys. Artillery, howitzer, horses and stretcher-bearers completed the scene.

Cannons boomed as cavalry units charged from the trees. Gunshot erupted and echoed through the city. Wisps of smoke spiraled upward forming vapor clouds as a commentator injected facts of bridges, bombardments, and the numbers of soldiers, both Union and Confederate, killed that day.

After the mock battle, as we returned to our car, we found ourselves strolling beside the "General" who was in charge of the troops, or enactment. Louis struck up a conversation with him. He said he was from Tennessee and had participated in thirty such programs through the years. He went on to say:

"My next duty is a trip to Gettysburg. I am to report on progress being made in raising funds for the erection of a memorial to honor soldiers from Tennessee who fought, and died, in the Battle of Gettysburg. We have discovered Tennessee is the only state whose men participated in that battle that has no memorial erected to its soldiers on the grounds, even though units from Tennessee opened and closed the battle. To this day, no reason has been found for this omission. In 1974 a bill was introduced, and passed, in our state legislature to support a monument. The cost was estimated at $ 175,000. The governor vetoed the bill."

I wondered about this conversation for several years. I finally researched the subject. In answer to my query, Bertram H. Barnett, Historian at the Gettysburg National Military Park, supplied the following information:

"The Tennessee State memorial was dedicated on July 3,1982 on the Gettysburg battlefield. It was the last of the Confederate states to erect a memorial. It honors Tennessians of Archer's Brigade which formed a portion of A.P. Hill's Corps of the Army of Virginia."

A pamphlet with pictured sections from David G. Martin's book titles "The Gettysburg Battle Monuments", Volume 1, was included. It stated that after the project was vetoed, Donald A. Ramsay Sr., of the Confederate High command, organized a commission to raise funds and to oversee the project for a monument. Nine years later it became a reality.

The original design, by the sculptor of the Iwo Jima memorial, Felix de Weldon, was to have featured three confederate soldiers, each 12 feet high. The actual monument is a black granite slab 6 feet tall bearing three soldiers and three ten inch gray marble stars, one for each Grand Division of Tennessee. This rests on a 16 feet long slab and signifies that Tennessee was the sixteenth state to join the Union. (1796) The cost was $25,000. All funds were raised through private contributions.

Once plans included a series of stepping stones leading to the monument. Each state was to donate $500.00 for the cost of these added attractions. Indiana contributed its part in 1979, as did the Confederate Historical Association of Belgium. No other states contributed. The steps were omitted.

The dedication ceremonies were conducted during a steady rain. Donald Ramsey Sr. delivered the speech. I have often wondered, could Donald Ramsey have been the general that we met at the re-enactment ceremony in Bluffton. I would like to think so.

Shortly after Hancel returned to Florida tragedy struck. Sis took the call. Willie had been killed in an automobile accident. The task of breaking the news to Hancel fell to her. Wondering how she would tell her mother that her son had died, she gave her a sedative. After a few minutes she gently said, "Mom, I have sad news to tell you," "I wondered why you gave me that pill. Has something happened to one of my children?"

Seeing a nod of affirmation, she cried, "Not Joseph?" Being the oldest it was only natural that she thought of him first.

"No. It's Willie."

"Oh No! Not Willie!" Had it been Louis she would have said not Louis, if me, she would have said, not Julia, for she loved one no greater than the other. The loss would have been as great no matter which one it was. But it was Willie, kind and gentle, sensitive and caring.

Nearing retirement age, he was looking forward to a few leisure years of traveling to new place; out of ordinary spaces. It was not to be. A passing truck spilled an object into the path of the car in which he was riding. The car spun out of control and hit a concrete bridge. Willie was killed instantly. His wife, Norma, barely escaped with her life.

Hancel would not return to Indiana to attend the funeral. She could not bury her son. Although a man grown, in her mind he was still her little boy. She wanted to remember him as he was growing up, sensitive, tending to worry, but gay and fun loving. The heartache lingered, never to dispel. But somehow she found the strength to get through it, as she always did.

She soon began inserting news items in her letters. Special clippings about Billy Carter, whose antics amused her. One article described the President as a God fearing man, modest and a refined gentleman. It alluded to Billy as the original good old boy, as southern as sawmill gravy, with a passion for strong drink and loafing around his service station with his buddies. Billy described himself as a red, white and blue patriot because he wore white socks, had a red neck, and drank Blue Ribbon beer.

After wintering in the Rio Grand Valley, we drove to Florida to pick Hancel up for her return trip to Indiana. We planned a surprise side trip to Plains, Georgia. Perhaps she would spy Billy. Seeing a sign pointing to Americus, she immediately guessed where we were going.

Arriving in Plains, the first thing we saw was a large mobile home being moved out of town. Billy was leaving Plains because he was tired of being gawked at. He was quoted as saying, "Having a brother for president is a sure way to mess up a home town."

Hancel didn't get to see Billy, but she saw the famous filling station. As we entered Hugh Carter's Antique store she pointed to the threshold. Feet that trampled and crossed it, through the years, had worn it thin. Visitors from every state, and from around the world, now tread those boards. A brisk business was being conducted selling peanut cookbooks, peanut candy, whimsical peanut men, and other odd characterizations, besides peanut butter and just plain peanuts.

We also visited the old depot being used as President Carter's campaign headquarters for the up-coming election. Tourist packed the streets so we didn't tarry long. We opted instead to spend our time touring the Andersonville National Park and Cemetery, a few miles away.

As we strolled among the markers Hancel reminisced about a tale her grandmother had told her, years ago, of a brother who was confined in a prison in South Carolina during the Civil War. He had contracted TB and was sent home to die. She hoped that prison had not been as dreadful as Andersonville was. Surrounded by blooming dogwood and Rose of Sharon, it is now a pleasant and serene setting for the final resting place of many "who gave their last full measure of devotion." A place that, despite the lovely blossoms, reminds me of another quotation, "War is Hell."

THEY WALTZED ALL OVER GOD'S HEAVEN

During the winter of 1978-79, while in Florida, Hancel fell and broke her hip. Enduring pain, she recuperated gradually. When it was time to return to Florida the next fall, for various reasons, Sis wrote that other arrangements would have to be made. Ned and I had already made reservations to return to Brownsville, Texas. Thinking that Hancel would enjoy it, I made reservations to rent a mobile home in the travel trailer court, along side of us, for her.

When Hancel learned of the arrangements, she refused to go, insisting that she would return to Florida, as usual. Finally convinced that the warmth of Texas was the alternative to the cold of Indiana, she agreed to go to Texas. Once reconciled to the plans, she looked forward to a new adventure. Ned and I proceeded to Texas, established our-selves and made things ready for her arrival. In November, accompanied by Louis's wife, Joan, Hancel flew down to join us.

She loved strolling around the court meeting new people and attending social functions. We though she would enjoy Mexico but one trip across the Rio Grande was enough for her. She loved the flowers and the markets but abhorred the poverty.

During a lull in activities, following the Christmas and New Years celebrations, she confined that she needed to see a doctor. The ominous diagnosis was cancer. Immediate surgery was scheduled. I concealed the fact that it was cancer.

The doctor assured me that the malignancy had all been eradicated. As Hancel improved she questioned the source of her problems. I repeated the doctor's prognosis. She accepted the situation stoically, as she had always accepted adversities during her life. She recuperated and bounced back with a resilience that belied her age.

On January 27, 1980 she celebrated her eighty-fifth birthday. We hosted a party with ice cream and cake, candles and gifts, surrounded by her new friends and neighbors. One of the guests was a retired railroad engineer from Logansport, Indiana. While conversing with him she mentioned the little farm where she once lived and related the story of how her children picked up coal along the tracks. From her description, he remembered having passed the property many times during his working years. Later, like a young nephew, he made it a point to stop for an occasional visit to reminisce with her.

On a follow up visit to the doctor, it was discovered the cancer had spread. A second surgery was necessary. Again we were amazed at her resilience. However, on the next visit I knew from the doctor's facial expression that the cancer was spreading.

I laid my hand on his shoulder and said, "Don't find anything. I must get my mother home."

"Yes, you must. Get her to a doctor immediately."

Flight arrangements were made, with assurance that she would receive special attention while in flight, and Louis would meet her in Indiana. We left for home immediately.

When we arrived home she was again hospitalized. The doctors had offered two options, immediate surgery or chemotherapy treatments. She refused surgery, and would make no commitment as to chemotherapy. As million of sons before had done, Louis was forced to make the imperative decision for her.

I arrived home in time to be with her for Mother's day. When she saw me she asked if I had received her letter. I had not, since it was only from habit that she thought she had written. When Joseph entered her hospital room her face lit up and she grasped his hand. Again Joseph was the one she was most elated to see. Kept sedated, she slipped quietly into death.

To ease my sadness, I visualized a beautiful young lady, clad in a white linen skirt and georgette blouse. As Heavens gates opened a handsome young Louie materialized.   He stepped forward, tipped his hat, and said, "Hancel, waltz with me." ——— And they danced all over God's Heaven.

Continues with ANCESTORS OF YORE

ANCESTORS OF YORE

I could rest upon my laurels after four score years — and then

Instead I seek out diverse subject to scribble with my pen.

I have no magic potion; no genie at my beck and call

To stipulate, or orchestrate a subject, theme, or genre

So with no minute directions etched on monument or cairn

I gravitate down a path once traveled, where memories dwell.

As I open wide an inner door they escape their prison cell,

Liberated specters, ancestors who lived in days of yore

Recognizable through family history, myth, and lore

Appear in cinematic replay, frame by frame.

I hasten to record them lest they wane.

PROLOGUE

After writing my memoirs, or "Hancel" the responses and questions generated by my children and grandchildren prompted me to research my ancestors. I quickly discovered that family history, like a crazy quilt, is compiled of handed down bits and pieces. Tales, repeated generation after generation, and accepted as facts, are often colorfully embellished, or exaggerated, making it difficult to distinguish myth from actually genealogical facts.

It's a fact that some of my ancestors crossed the Cumberland Gap in a covered wagon, but in tracing family genealogy the trail often became as twisted as the pike that crossed the mountains. However, Chappel Clan members were among the first settlers in Indiana.

I puzzled which tales to include. Suppose I unearth a weasel in the woodpile. Should I disclose it? I concluded no one would object to a few century old skeletons. As in good cooking, a little spice constitutes the difference between ordinary viands and gourmet food.

Contemplating my search, I remembered an article published in the Logansport Pharos Tribune a few years ago. It stated that during a cleanup project at the old Ninth Street Cemetery a number of fallen down, and dilapidated, tombstones led to the discovery of several Revolutionary War soldier's graves. Among the names listed from the old markers I recognized one as that of a long ago ancestor. With this as a focal point to begin my quest, I went in search of his burial site.

JULIA V. DAWSON

SAMUEL CHAPPEL

As I wondered among the headstones, I met the sexton. Through his records I located a bronze plaque, supplied by the government to the old veterans for their long ago service. They had been obtained through the efforts of a local historian. The one I sought read:

> SAMUEL CHAPPEL
> Born Feb. 2, 1792 - Died Jan. 9, 1839
> War of 1812
> CAPTAIN Aug. 20, 1821 — Indiana

With that bit of information I was hooked! Samuel Chappel was my great, great, grandfather. The birth date showed that he was born five years after the Constitutional Convention met and created the United States of America. He would have been three years old when George Washington became president. That year, elsewhere in the world, Marie Antoinette and Louis XVI of France were guillotined.

I also discovered the records of the gravesites of Stephen Chappel, my great grandfather, and that of his wife, Elizabeth. Stephen and Elizabeth were the parents of William, who was Hancel's father, in the preceding tale. The records disclosed a toddler, Samuel age two years, died two days before another son, Austin, was born and that the couple also buried a young daughter, Martha. With one stop I discovered three more branches on the family tree.

Another interesting bit of information listed on the printout sheet from the sexton's office read: William Cooley died Dec. 18/1853 at the age of fifty-three years and eleven days. Cooley was the body servant of General Andrew Jackson at the Battle of

New Orleans. For his devotion, Jackson granted him his freedom. He is buried at the Ninth Street Cemetery.

The friendly sexton interjected that the first settlers had been interred near the old trading post from which the city of Logansport, Indiana evolved. The bodies were later exhumed and transferred to the new Spier Spenser Square Cemetery when it was established in 1848. That cemetery sat on the SE corner of Market and Ninth Street, where the present day post office is now located. Today the site is marked with a small sign that reads: The Spier Spencer Square. It was named in honor of Captain Spencer who fought in the Battle of Tippecanoe. Few townspeople realize that the site was once a graveyard.

Within a year the growth of the community prompted the Ninth Street Cemetery to be established. At that time all remains were transferred to that location. When the Mount Hope Cemetery was dedicated many remains were again moved to that site. As the sexton related this history he commented, "John Tipton, the man known as the Father of Logansport, got around about as much in death as he did in life."

Enthralled by his tales, my next stop was a trip to the library. As I delved into past history of the area, I discovered: that John Tipton served as a young Lieutenant in the Battle of Tippecanoe. He figured in many activities of early Cass County. After establishing a trading post in the area he was appointed Indian Agent by President Monroe. At first Tipton had no love for the Indians. Cherokee in Tennessee massacred his father in 1793. When land on the new frontier was allotted, Tipton became Land Agent.

Early settlers pitched their tents and built cabins around an Indian village, called Ki-na-pa-com-a-qua, near the Eel and the Wabash Rivers. "The French called it L'Aquille. Wigwams stretched from the east side of Twelve Mile Creek into Adams Township.

* Powell's History of Cass County vol. 1

Records show that as early as 1748, fourteen families lived at Fort Quiatenon, near present day Lafayette; eighty families lived near Post Vincennes; and ten lived at the confluence of the St Mary and St. Joseph Rivers.

The first land opened for settlement in the area know as the Northwest Territory, or Indian Territory, was granted to the Ohio Company. In 1748 King George II, hoping to create and reap benefits from fur trade and to establish forts in the region, set aside 500,000 areas on the upper Ohio River; 200.000 acres south of the river along the Kanawha and the Monongahela Rivers; and 300.000 on both sides of the Ohio. The Ohio Company was composed of wealthy Virginians who received land grants, in specified numbers of acres, for each settler they induced to move to the regions. This was land acquired by the English in 1682 and ceded to the colonies in 1784. It was under the jurisdiction of Virginia.

As early as 1791 white settlers from Virginia and Kentucky joined troops from Fort Washington and marched through dense forests to the Wabash River. They crossed the river seven miles east of present day Logansport and destroyed an Indian village.

A land rush began in 1783, after the Revolutionary War. Youth fresh from the war received land grants in payment for war service. Veterans flocked over the Cumberland, down the Ohio, across the mountains, and along the Wilderness Trail. They migrated from New York, Maryland, Pennsylvania, New Jersey, North Carolina, and Kentucky. They settled along the Big Sandy, the Middle River. Coal Water, Tug Creek, and the Scioto.

** Pioneer Families of E. and SE Kentucky, by Kozee — continues:

By 1782 a land rush began in Kentucky. As many as 8,000 to 10,000 came, Anglo Saxons, Huguenots, Scotch and Irish. Many settled in White Springs in what is now Madison and Washington Counties in Indiana.

The first Indian treaty affecting Indiana land was in 1795; land ceded by Indians at Fort Recovery, Ohio. This opened for settlement six years later and a land office was established in Cincinnati. In the meantime, settlers entered the area as squatters. On September 4,1820 a land office opened in Crawfordsville and one in Terra Haute. —(Interestingly, that was the same year Samuel Chappel was made Captain in Indiana.) Land sold at auction included that in southern Indiana, Kentucky, Tennessee, and Pennsylvania. The Terra Haute office closed May 31/1823, listing #01459 on the last receipt. Crawfordsville reopened the sales with #01460 on June 5/1823. It remained open until Sept. 7/1829 with it's final sale on March 26,1853. Unsold land was attached to the Indianapolis land office. Sales were recorded in The Tract or Land Entry Book, listing dates, buyers name and address, and location of the land office, and the amount paid.

During the first decades of government land sales in Indiana three hundred and twenty acres were sold, by the section or quarter sections, for $1.25 per acre, a price set by Congress. Through nine treaties, signed between 1795 and 1854, the Indians were paid from five cents to seven cents per acre. Often it was a mere penny an acre. Land sold at auctions, to the highest bidder, sold for $2.00 per acre. In 1830 to 1840 Congress gave the squatters an opportunity to buy their land at a minimum price.

John Tipton, supposedly the first white man in the area, built his cabin and trading post in 1828. The settlement became know as Olde town. A trail led to the old White Post, on the Tippecanoe River, where the city of Monticello in White Co. is now located. Another trail led to Lake Michigan and on to Illinois.

An Indian village lay about two miles south of where Lewisburg was established. It was called Old Sally's Village, named for an old Indian squaw. This became the meeting place where Tipton, as Indian agent, meted out annual payments to the

Indians.   Tribe after tribe was forced to sign treaties relinquishing their lands, as mentioned above. Indian chiefs who signed treaties were exempt from being forced to leave their lands.

According to old newspaper reports, the first child born in Olde Town made it's appearance on December 30/ 1821. (The same year Samuel Chappel's son, Stephen was born in Virginia.) Olde Town, seven miles east of present day Logansport, became known as Logan's Port in honor of Chief Logan who remained a friend of the white settlers. The name was selected as the result of a shooting match.   Official, the name later became Logansport, one word.

    * Sources: Researched through articles from Indiana Magazines of History, and "Histories of Cass County "by Helms, and from articles written by Powell and Tipton.

CHIEF LOGAN

Continuing my research, I pursued the history of Chief Logan. I remembered a long ago gift of books that Hancel had received from her grandmother, Paulina Dora Ward Kirk, and which were passed on to me. Knowing one of the books contained orations by famous Indians, I examined each book volume and found the following information, and speech delivered by Chief Logan:

Logan, a Cayuga, was made chief of the Mingoes. His family lived in Pennsylvania where they were all murdered in a skirmish between Indians and a whiskey trader, named Greathouse. Logan's Indian name was Tahgahjuta. He took the name Logan from a general who befriended him when he was a small boy. Thinking that the American troops were responsible for the murder of his entire family, and forced from his homeland to the western frontier, Logan fought and led other Indian tribes in the Battle of Point Pleasant during Lord Dunmore's War. Dunmore was the governor of Virginia. Logan was credited with taking thirty scalps in that battle. After peace was established, he gave the following oration:

"No white man ever entered Logan's cabin hungry, and he gave him not meat. If he was cold and naked, I clothed him. During the course of the long bloody war Logan remained in his cabin, an advocate of peace. Such was my love and friendship with the white man that my countrymen pointed to me and said, 'Logan is a friend of the white man.'

Last spring, in cold blood, all my family was murdered not even sparing women or children. There runs not a drop of my blood in any living creature. I sought revenge. I have glutted that revenge. Now I rejoice for peace in my country. But Logan never felt fear. Logan will not turn on his heel to save his Life. Who is left to mourn Logan? Not one."

* Source: "THE WORLD'S FAMOUS ORATIONS." by Wm. Jennings Bryant, published in 1906. Logan's speech was in Vol.VII - America 1774 -1837

Savannah Indians, for whom the Savanna River and the city in Georgia were named, and various tribes of the southeast, from Tennessee and Florida, were gradually pushed as far as the headquarters of the Ohio River by advancing pioneers. By 1768 these settled along the Scioto and Miami Rivers. They gradually united into one tribe and became known as the Shawnee, or "the people of the south." The following facts gleaned along the way were not pertinent to my genealogy research, but I found them interesting enough to note. These tid-bits of history only make the searching more interesting.

Tipton built a fur trading post on land still known as the N.W. Territory. At a ferry crossing in Logansport, during those early days, passenger fare was six and one-half cents. A horse cost eighteen and one-quarter cents; an ox was twelve and one-half cents; sheep and pigs cost three cents; a wagon -fifty cents; and a man on horseback was twenty-five cents. Half cents were paid in mills, with ten mills in a cent. The first Temperance movement in Cass County was organized in 1829. The first Anti-Saloon League was formed in 1831 with John Tipton as acting president.

Prior to 1800 the only land owned by individuals in what is now Indiana was either in Vincennes, where the title went back to the French; Indian land grants, or in Clark's Grant which was opposite to present day Louisville. This consisted of land allotted to men who served with George Rogers Clark during the Revolutionary War.

Tipton, born in Virginia in 1786, was a mounted rifleman in a company known as the Yellow Jackets. Before acting as Indian agent in Logansport he served in that capacity at Fort Wayne, Indiana. According to the Early History of Carroll County by Helms. "It was the Indian Agency and the Indian trade that made Logansport. It brought men of enterprise and capital. Also, its location on the Michigan road gave it prominence." Other historical accounts noted that many pioneers entered the territory via the old Quaker trace, passing through Richmond, Indiana. As they did so, settlers advised, "You'll die if you go to the Wabash. Everyone who goes there is dead in less than a year." An old timer from Carroll County, a Dr. John M. Ewing, noted,

"In 1827, where the town of Logansport now stands there was a dense hazel and blackberry thicket. There were no roads, only deer paths and snakes a plenty, big rattlesnakes. Settlers spotted their dens and killed them in the spring when they came out." Carroll County was organized in 1828. It included the territory now encompassed in Cass and White Counties. In 1827 there were only forty families living in the areas of what is now Carroll, Cass, and Whites Counties. Cass became a county in 1829, and by 1831 the settlement that became Logansport had seven hundred inhabitants.

My next quest was the Cass County courthouse.

A VISIT TO THE CASS COUNTY COURT HOUSE

Disappointment. I quickly learned that no birth or death records existed until 1874, when a health department was established. I also learned there were very few records for veterans of the War of 1812. So I headed for the Recorder's office to check land records.

With a heavy tome laid atop a desk, about level with my eyes, I searched for information while standing on tiptoes, only to discover that land records didn't begin until 1840. But, having worked as a real-estate sales lady (Lake and Porter Co.) for several years, I knew that old abstracts of titles and land descriptions could be interesting for the history they revealed, so I continued to search.

As I browsed, I recognized names of land purchasers in Cass County as those I had encountered in the above mention northern Indiana counties. One early purchaser that I especially remember was George Ewing, who has a subdivision in Hobart named for him. Considering transportation modes back then, horseback, wagon, buggy or shanks mare, I marveled how land speculators roamed so far a field. But with no super-highways to confine them, they could go as the crow flies and minimized the mileage.

Old land descriptions listed land as "being in a line with a hackberry pole, 2inches in diameter, N. so many degrees, W. by a number of links to a hickory elm tree, thence 6 links to a Burr oak, 12 acres more or less." Survey crews actually drug huge chains around the country measuring metes and bounds: 1 link = 8 inches, 25 links = 1 rod, and 4 rods = 1 chain. Those old markers of trees and hedges, as boundary markers, often disappeared with time.

One old description read, "As being a section of land situated on the Wabash River in Cass County, being a section granted to Chin-Qua-Qua, or Duck. This was granted in a treaty made between the United States Government and the Miami Indians. It was further described as Duck Section. One that adjoins land granted to Black Loon, belonging to the Miami Tribe of Indians: containing two sections, or 128 acres, by treaty of November 6, 1838, embracing the falls of Pipe Creek.

Three sections of land, 1920 acres, deeded in 1839 sold for the consideration of $10,000. One 12-acre tract sold for $1200.00. Others sale prices were recorded as low as fifty cents per acre. I gained no genealogy from this information, but I was intrigued by the historical facts, so I continued searching.

In 1788, Congress set aside 100,000 acres of land on both sides of the Wabash River, across from present day Louisville, in Illinois Country. It was known as the Vincennes Tract, reserved for George Rogers Clark, to be allotted to men who had served under him in the Revolutionary War.

In 1800, by an act of Congress, the Indiana Territory was established with Vincennes as it's capital. It embraced the present day states of Illinois, Wisconsin, Upper Michigan, part of Minnesota, and Indiana. Land that once belonged to the Miami Confederation, namely the Algonquin, Twightwees, Weas, Shockeyes, and Pisneshaws; tribes that banded together for protection against the Iroquois. The Miami Confederation extended from the Scioto River to the Great Lakes and west to Illinois. Their villages strung from along the St. Joseph, the St. Mary, Maumee, and the Wabash Rivers. They called the Wabash Wah-bah-shik-ki. Gradually the Pottawatomis were driven south by the Iroquois and became known as the Prairie and Wabash Pottawatomi.

The Pottawatomi, Miami, Weas, and Delaware Indians ceded land west of the Tippecanoe River in 1818, and in 1826 Indiana purchased a one hundred foot strip of land from the Pottawatomis for construction of the Michigan Road. It was to run from Lake Michigan to Indianapolis, and continue on to a point on the Ohio River. The Indians were paid $2,000 silver, to be prorated over a twenty years. They would also receive $2,000 annually to educate their children; a mill to grind their corn; a miller to operate the mill; and 160 bushels of salt. Blacksmith shops would be built at intervals along the road. By 1836 the Pottawatomi agreed to migrate to a reservation within two years. By 1872 all tribal land in Indiana was extinguished.

Before the white man came the Indians were free to roam where they pleased, from the Land of the Sky Blue Waters to the Big Sky Country. They followed the buffalo and the deer, which fed and clothed them. Wherever they built their fires and pitched their wigwams the land became theirs, unless another tribe had erected their tents before them. Often battles had to be fought to protect their turf from warring tribes, like the above-mentioned Iroquois.

It was not only the coming of the white settlers that changed the Indians lives forever. It was the extinction of the buffalo herds. As late as 1790 buffalo herds roamed Indiana. Then, for some unknown reason the winters became more severe. Snow, ice, and rain covered their grazing lands. The animals died in great numbers. Those that did not starve, or were killed by hunters, migrated across the Mississippi River. The great buffalo traces in southern Indiana became travel routes for the pioneers. One of those early pioneers was my great, great grandfather, Samuel Chappel.

By 1820-1830 Congress set the price of land at $1.25 per acre. It was divided into tiers and townships through the foresight of Thomas Jefferson. As early as 1827, land was auctioned from the steps of Washington Hall in Logansport, in limits of one section of land, at $1.25 an acre. Washington Hall was the first hotel, or tavern, that was built in the rapidly growing Logansport, consisting of "A cluster of cabins and a few real frame homes." Chanucey Carter laid out the original town site, 122 lots, with the east terminus being Fifth Street. By 1827 the community had a post office.

I especially noted an entrée, dated 12/1839, granting land to the trustees of Indian Creek Church to erect a Presbyterian meetinghouse and burial grounds. My interest stemmed from the fact that members of the Newbraugh family might be interred there. Elizabeth Newbraugh, William's mother and my great-grandmother. This was a lead I had been going to pursue.

A VISIT TO THE WHITE COUNTY COURTHOUSE

Thinking I might find records of my great grandmother, of whom Hancel had spoken so often, I headed to the White County courthouse in Monticello, Indiana. I began with the birth records but found that none existed until after 1882. Before that White County, as well as Cass, were a part of Carroll County until 1847-48.

Here, I found the first twist in the handed down tales. Hancel had always referred to her grandmother as Grandma Kirk. Old marriage records listed her maiden name as Ward. The name Kirk was acquired through a second marriage. The 1860 census of Round Grove Township, White County, listed Austin Ward's family, including a daughter, Paulina Dora Ward, age fifteen, born in Indiana in 1845. Marriage records showed that on July 30, 1874 Paulina married Nash Anderson. Later records disclosed that on March 16,1881 she wed Edward J. Kirk. - Thus the name Kirk became a family name with Willie's middle name being Kirk. I soon discovered that the names Anderson, Ward, Kirk and Chappel were all entwined in my heritage. I could not find the death records of Nash Anderson; in fact no further data of any kind. This might indicated that they were divorced. I did determine that Edward J. Kirk died in Jasper County in 1891. Paulina Kirk was listed in the Jasper County census in 1900, as were William and Sadie Chappel and their family. Hancel had often spoken of growing up in Jasper County.

Later, I discovered an old picture of Paulina and Aunt Vi, as a young girl, standing in front of a newly constructed church in Upland, in Grant County. The picture was not dated, but later records listed William and Sadie, and family, in the 1910 census of Jefferson Township, Grant Co. Dora was not listed but the old picture, the near fire incident, and numerous mentioning of her, indicated she moved with them. Her paper trail seemed to end.

Remembering Grandma Sadie's tale of how she was united with a long sister, Minnie, and having visited Minnie at her home in rural Monticello, I checked record for her. Book 28, page 51, at the White County Health Department lists her born August 1/1870. Liberty Township; Mother, Paulina Dora Ward - Father, unknown. Minnie married Wallace Moore of White Co. 1/12/1865 in Carroll Co. It listed their children's births. Child # 1 was born June 5/ 1898; no record of gender; no name recorded. Except for a stillborn infant, the others were girls, whom I had met. Minnie died Sept. 4,1935.

Remembering the tale of Minnie's son, Lonnie, killed in World War I, and assuming the child listed as her first-born, unidentified by name or gender, but of an age to have fought in that war, I headed for the Veterans Administration office. I found no record, but was informed that he could have enlisted, and been discharged, from another county. I drew another blank. But as is often the case, I came up a bit of interesting information.

The day before my visit to the courthouse, November 4, 1997, the last remaining White County veteran of World War I had died at the age of 104 years. I did not note his name.

As I conversed with the lady in charge of the veteran's office, I mentioned how I had discovered the bronze marker on my great, great grandfather's grave. She said although the government once furnished them to all soldiers, honorably discharged or to those with unmarked graves, they no longer do so. If a family can purchase a marker, or erect a stone, none is forthcoming from the government.

A few days later I returned to Monticello and continued my search at the White County Historical Museum. Here, I hit a bonanza! Contacting the genealogist, I informed her that I was seeking information about the Austin Ward family. She said there were many Wards in the area. Nothing rang a bell until I mentioned Granville Ward, listed in an old census as Paulina's brother. With the mention of Granville, her face lit up.

"Molly! Do you know Molly?" At a nod in the negative from me she continued.

"Molly was Granville's daughter. I interviewed her, several years ago, as she was about to celebrate her 100th birthday. She was confined in a local nursing home, and was almost totally deaf. I carried a large artist sketchpad upon which I could scribble questions for her to answer. Although she could not hear, she possessed an astute memory for details. The nurse cautioned that I should not tire her, and to make my visit short. She came often instructing me to leave as I was tiring Molly. Molly chased her away every time."

The hour was getting late. It was time for the museum to close. Workers were departing and doors were being locked. We moved outside and stood by my car conversing. We finally decided that I must return another day. In the interim, she promised to locate a file that Molly had donated to the museum.

GRANVILLE WARD

A few days later I retuned to the museum. As the genealogist related Molly's story she handed me a large manila envelope to examine. It contained pictures, newspaper clipping, and sundry items accumulated through the years by Molly. Molly and my grandmother, Sadie, would have been cousins. The following is her father, Granville Ward's, story as I discovered it that day:

Granville was ten years old when his family arrived in White County. He helped his father till the family farm with a pair of oxen. In later years he attended the State University at Bloomington, Indiana in the winter, and worked on the farm during the summer. When the Civil War broke out, Granville and his friend, Jim Rawlins, went to Indianapolis and enlisted in the 14th. Indiana Volunteer Infantry; the first regiment mustered in Indiana. Granville rose to the rank of Captain.

He fought in the battles of Gettyburg, Fredericksburg, and Chancellorsville.

During the Battle of Chancellorsville Granville was shot from his horse. He lay on the battlefield all day, shot through the knee and in excruciating pain. When night fell, although in agony, he crawled toward his army's lines. At nightfall, when the firing had ceased, some of his men found him. They carried him to a nearby barn, whose owner was known to be a Northern sympathizer. Making him as comfortable as possible, his comrades departed, leaving Granville, as they thought, in safety.

The next morning the wife of the barn owner discovered him and notified his commander. He sent soldiers to get Granville. They put him, along with other wounded soldiers, on a freight train to be transported to a hospital near Washington, D.C.

Granville laid in the hospital as doctors tried to save his leg. Surgeons were in short supply and none knew how to remove the bullet lodged in the knee joint. Gradually, gangrene began to develop. Granville suffered greatly. Finally after twenty-seven days, with limited knowledge, doctors were forced to amputate the leg in order to save his life.

The Surgeon General had issued an edict to Union medical officers to preserve specimens of anatomies with projectiles, and foreign bodies, removed from the wounded that might lend themselves of use in medical studies. Surgery of the knee joint had never been attempted. Since it would be of interest to the medical profession, the knee was saved. It remained on display at the Smithsonian Museum for many years.

Lincoln often visited the wounded. One day, as he made his rounds, the nurses asked him to visit the young man from Indiana, as he was surely going to die. Lincoln found Granville's bed. Realizing the dire circumstances of Granville's condition, and aware of the lack of nurses, Lincoln asked, "Do you have a mother?"

Granville answered, "Yes, and I know if she were here to take care of me, I would get well."

Lincoln asked, "Do you think she would come and care for you?"

With his answer in the affirmative, Lincoln sent Granville's mother a message. "Your son is critically wounded. The hospital is filled with wounded. There are few to administer the constant care that your son will need. Could you come and nurse your son back to health? A ticket will be waiting for you at the train station."

Granville's mother journeyed to the hospital. She was issued blankets and a pillow. She made a pallet on the floor beside her son's cot. She tended him, night and day, for about six weeks, until he resigned his captaincy. My old copy of his army discharge states: Granville B. Ward, Capt, Co. K - 14 Ind. Vol. Inft. was wounded at the battle of Chancellorsville, VA. May 3rd. 1863. In consequences of said wound Capt. G.B, Ward resigns his position in the (14th) Regt. Signed: Gen.W.M. Cume,

Surgeon. It is dated Feb. 5/ 1864. Headquarters 14Th. Ind. Inft. At a camp near Sharpsburg. (?) The old ink on the hand written document is difficult to decipher, having faded through the years.

After he resigned, Granville and his mother boarded a train for the return trip to Indiana. On the way home, his mother became ill. They got off the train in Pittsburgh, Pa. Having contracted typhoid fever at the hospital while nursing her son, his mother, Elizabeth, died. Austin Ward sorrowfully went to bring home his injured son and the body of his dead wife.

Austin also lost another son, William Ward, and Granville's youngest brother, who had enlisted in the 10th Indiana Volunteer Infantry. He was captured and sent to prison, in South Carolina. He contracted T.B. and was sent home. He died shortly after returning home. (Hancel had alluded to this soldier when we toured the Andersonville prison. I had, however, never heard Granville's tale.)

Another bit of information I gleaned when trying to research the Battle of Chancellorsville. It was in that battle that Stonewall Jackson fell, mortally wounded, shot accidentally by his own troops. He died eight days later. General Robert E. Lee is quoted as having said, "Jackson lost his leg but I lost my right hand man." * Source: Civil War Battle Encyclopedia.

Grandville was fitted with a wooden leg. He returned to school in Bloomington. In May 1864 he married Catherine C. Rowlins, the sister of Jim Rowlins who had accompanied him to Indianapolis when they enlisted in the war. In 1864 he was elected as Treasurer of White County. He was re-elected in 1866. He served as postmaster in Monticello from 1889 to 1893.

He was active in the GAR, Grand Army of the Republic, composed of members of the Army, Navy and Marine Corps who served in the War of Rebellion from April12, 1861 to April 9, 1865, and having been honorably discharged. No one who had ever bore arms against the United States could join. The GAR was organized in Decatur, Ill. three years after the close of the Civil War. When Indiana's post was founded thirty veterans attended. One year later, a National encampment was held in Indianapolis. (Remember the old GAR booklet that had been found among Hancel's papers?) At that meeting the following resolution was passed: All flags hoisted on Memorial Day shall fly at half-mast to honor our fallen comrades. A tradition was established. Granville and his wife raised seven children.

An old clipping found in Molly's envelope, contained the following information about their son, James: "James A. Ward, general manager of National Power Company of Casper, Wyo., who was commissioned 1st. Lieutenant, Engineer Corp. of the United States Army, will leave for camp, in France, in three weeks. Jim was a member of Capt. Guthrie's Company in the Spanish American War." Another bit of interesting news, saved through the years by Molly, told how Jim had established that electric company in Wyoming and how it was destroyed by fire. Although Jim's financial loses were great, he was able to recoup and carry on the business.

Shortly after Granville married, his father died. Following the death of his first wife Austin remarried and acquired three stepchildren. At his father's death, Granville assumed responsibility of raising his two younger sisters and the stepchildren. As difficult as it was tending the farm with his disabilities, Granville managed. But raising the girls proved too much for him, so they were "taken in" by various family members. This may explain the separation of Sadie and Minnie.

Later research disclosed a Minerva Ward (Minnie) Minerva Chappel, and a Minerva Kirk. I believe the later was the little girl who was lost in the long ago travels from North Carolina. Records show that the Kirks were from N.C. and settled in what is Jasper County in the 1800s. Or it simply may be that my childhood memories were fuzzy.

With the aid of his wife's three brothers, Granville built a new home. Molly had even included a picture of it. In time, Granville established a touring business in Chicago, escorting tourists around the town by horse and carriage. Being my great grandmother's brother, he would have been my great uncle.

MOLLY 1873 - 1977

As I scanned the contents of Molly's envelope I found several pictures of her. She was beautiful, not only physically but also in soul, as I would learn. Her beauty was documented by the fact that she took first prize as the most beautiful baby at the first White County Fair, held in 1874. She was depicted as a lovely mature young lady, and also in her senior years.

After listening to her father's war tales, especially the lack of trained medical personnel, Molly decided she would be a nurse. She enrolled in nursing classes in Chicago, where she lived with family friends. On her first day in training she was left in charge of an extremely ill patient. She was handed a chart and pen and issued instructions to watch the man closely; to keep him in bed, and write down all his actions and anything he might say. Later, when the instructor came to relieve her and to read the notes, Molly had scribbled, "Fit, bad fit! - He shook all over." Later she wrote, "He went to sleep." The nurse checked the man's pulse and found that he was dead. Molly was so frightened that she ran all the way home. For days she refused to return to classes. Finally, her friends convinced her to resume her studies.

One evening, while in training, Molly joined a group of friends attending a theatrical production. When the show was over, she accompanied friends backstage to meet the cast, especially the male singer and star performer, Billy Butler. Billy was a suave, handsome man of the world, somewhat in character with another Butler, Rhett Butler in Gone With The Wind. Billy invited the girls out for an after theater party. During the evening most of his attention was devoted to Molly. Molly was captivated by his debonair manners and flowery speech. She was swept off her feet in a whirlwind romance and soon accepted Billy's proposal of marriage.

In a short time, Billy moved on, treading the boards from coast to coast, leaving Molly behind. Billy's visits home became few and far between. In time, Molly found herself pregnant. The child was stillborn. Weeks turned into months with Billy away, literally abandoning Molly. She finally concluded their marriage was not working. She went to court, stood up, and announced to the judge that she wanted to obtain a divorce, but could not afford to pay a costly attorney fee. A young lawyer arose and volunteered to represent her, adding that he would make his charges fit her purse. That man was Clarence Darrow!

I immediately though of the famous Monkey Trial, in which Clarence Darrow represented Stokes for teaching evolution in a Tennessee school, and was opposed by attorney William Jennings Bryant. Intrigued, and wondering if it could be the same Clarence Darrow, I began to research him. I found the following information:

Clarence Darrow was born in Kineman, Ohio on April 18, 1857. He attended law school for only a year before becoming "a lawyer before the bar." In 1878 he moved to Chicago and became a partner with John P. Altgeed. This placed him in the right place at the right time. In time he was appointed City Corporation Counselor, General Attorney for the city of Chicago, and the Northwestern Railroad Co.; a position he resigned in order to defend Eugene V. Debs, President of the Railroad Union, and other officials in the Pullman strike of 1895. His other celebrated cases included the Leopold and Loeb trial. He was a well-known debater and public speaker. He is most remembered for defending Scopes for teaching the Darwinian Theory of Evolution in 1925. It was also interesting to note that, a one-time partner was poet Edgar Lee Masters, who wrote the "Spoon River Elegy."

Molly resumed her nursing career and became a surgical nurse, a rarity in her days, and her services were much in demand. She nursed soldiers on American bases during the

Spanish American War. Her career took her to five states and produced many stories, like the following:

One day a surgeon called Molly asking her to assist him in his first gall bladder operation. She traveled by train to Illinois where he met her. Upon her arrival, the doctor informed her that the surgery would have to be performed at the patient's rural home since there were no hospitals in the area.

Arriving at the farmhouse, Molly set about scrubbing the kitchen table, upon which the operation would be performed. For sanitary purposes she scoured the surrounding area and boiled all instruments that would be used in the surgery. The boiling and sterilizations of the paraphernalia was done on an old kitchen range. It was mid-August when the temperature soared.

Molly helped the doctor into his gown and mask. As the anesthetic was being administered the sweat dripped from the surgeon's brow. The air was stifling and the physician became faint. He told Molly that he could not precede under such conditions; a cooler, more airy, place would have to be found. Family members picked up the table, bearing the patient, and carried it into the yard under the shade of a large tree. The surgery was concluded with no problems. The patient survived and lived a long life.

In time, Molly married Dr. Henry Griest of Monticello, Indiana. They converted their home into a private hospital, the first hospital in the city. The big white frame house is still standing. For years Dr. Griest had dreamed of becoming a missionary doctor among primitive people. In 1920 the Board of National Missions of the Presbyterian Church approached him to go to Point Barrow, Alaska to build and operate a hospital. At first Molly, being pregnant, did not relish going to Alaska. But they went, and served faithfully for several years. During their years of working among the Eskimos the Griests entertained Captain Roland Amundsen, explorer, and Charles and Anne Lindbergh.

They were also official weather observers. When Wiley Post, accompanied by Will Rogers, radioed from Fairbanks that they were heading to Point Barrows. Dr. Griest advised them that it was unsafe to fly the eight hundred miles due to extreme fog. For four days they supplies Post with weather reports every two hours. On the fifth day, ignoring conditions and unknown to the Geiests, Post proceeded. Having made the trip twice before, no doubt he felt confident in his abilities. Later the missionaries learned that Post had over-passed the area. When he entered a cleared spot, over a small cabin and a land locked lake, he circled, descended, and taxied to the shore where an Eskimo family lived. Post and Rogers stood on the planes pontoons and called to the Eskimo, Okpoeka and his wife, asking for directions. Okpoeka, who spoke English, directed them, "15 miles northwest to Point Barrow." Post chose to fly on. He circled the lake trying for altitude, and to avoid thick fog. The plane rose sixty feet into the air. The engine sputtered and died and the plane plunged, nose first, into four feet of water and into the frozen gravel lake bottom. The engine crashed into the cockpit, demolished the plane, and killed Wiley Post and Will Rogers.

The Eskimos walked to Point Barrow and announced, "Plane fall. Two men killed." Since Post would have been expected from another direction, the Griest didn't suspect it to be him until another group arrived and told them; "One man has a sore eye. He was wearing a bandage over eye." The Griests knew then that it was Wiley Post. As they gathered medical supplies, and made ready to travel to the site, another group of Eskimos towing sleds arrived bearing the bodies. It took five hours to repair external wounds and to make the bodies presentable for loved ones. Acting on behalf of the two widows, Col. Charles Lindbergh arrived to escort the remains back to the states.

The wrecked plane was taken to Barrow where visitors, arriving by ship, began breaking it apart for souvenirs. To prevent this, the plane was burned.

Dr. Griest retired from the mission in 1938, at age seventy, after serving for eighteen years. He traveled and lectured for two more years before returning to Monticello, where he reopened his office, assisted by Molly. Sadly. Austin Ward, Molly's grandfather died while they were in Alaska. The Griest both loved the North Country. They loved reciting tales about how polar bears invaded the thousand miles of territory. They often traveled the barren coast by dogsled and always carried a gun. They treated the sick and preached to groups gathered in, or around, igloos in temperatures ranging to 60 degrees below zero. Surprisingly, no one had colds until infected by visitors. Their hearing was impaired by the cold, and their vision by the suns glare on the snow. Their diet consisted mostly of reindeer meat.

Molly wrote of her experiences in a book titles "Nursing Under The North Star." Even as a child she was an aspiring author. Included in the material she donated to the museum was a small booklet, made of sheets of yellow paper from a lined school tablet. It related her childish account of the great Chicago fire. Molly lived to be one hundred and three years of age. Many artifacts and Eskimo dolls the Griests had collected were sold, and donated, to the Children's Museum in Indianapolis, Indiana.

AUSTIN WARD

The first record I found of Austin Ward, my great, great grandfather, was in the 1860 census of White County. It listed him as a farmer. He was born in Virginia and his wife, Elizabeth Buskirk, came from Kentucky. Also listed were six children, including fifteen-year-old Paulina Dora, my great grandmother and Grandma Sadie's mother. They lived in Monroe County before migrating to White County in 1850, where they settled on a 200-acre farm. A Township was formed in 1858. At Austin's suggestion, it was named Round Grove Township for the circular grove of trees that grew in its southwest corner.

It was from that grove of trees that early settlers obtained logs to build their cabins. The Great Prairie began at the edge of the forest. Austin drove his bobsled, pulled by horses, to transport logs from the grove to build their first home, a 16 X 18 log cabin. They could see for miles across the flat land and often saw fox, deer, and prairie chickens.

Records showed that the first school erected was also a 16 x 18 cabin. Round Grove Township's first election was held there in 1858. Austin Ward was appointed "Inspector." He was Township Trustee for several years. The first bride married in the township was his daughter, Jane Ward.

Following Elizabeth's death, Austin remarried. The 1870 census listed his new wife as Unica, age 52, three stepchildren, a female named Kansas, and two males, Graham and Albert. All were born in Ohio. It also included Paulina Dora, daughter age 27 living at home. (She first married in1874) An item copied from the Standard History of White County, dated 1915, page 309 noted that Austin retired to Brookston, Indiana in 1873. He was a member of the Christian Church. He also served as Justice of the Peace.

I scribbled many notes during my research, but regretfully, for many I omitted the source. Probably because, at the time, I considered them trivia but now deem relevant to the era and interesting enough to share, such as: When cholera epidemics occurred people packed up their possessions and fled to new locations to avoid contact with neighbors who might spread the plague. Often what would have become a thriving community fell into obscurity because of this.

In 1800 there was an average of 104.2 acres for each man, woman, and child in the United States. By 1870, with the population at forty million, that figure dropped to 48 acres. By 1900 it was 25 acres.

When Indiana became a state, in 1816, a law was enacted to provide school districts and school buildings. It required "that every able bodied male person, age 21 or over, within their school districts, shall be liable for one days work each week until the school buildings are completed, or they shall pay thirty-seven and one-half cents per day for failing to work. In lieu of labor, or daily wages, he may supply the trustee with nails, lumber, glass or other building material."

Norway, Indiana, Election Notice: 12/28/1893: Any person who has not been vaccinated for smallpox will not be allowed to vote in the election. - Interestingly enough, my search for an earlier ancestor unearthed the information that the first smallpox inoculation, performed by Cotton Mather in 1721, was done under the guidance of his slave, Onesimus who learned the process from tribal medicine men in Africa. One more bit of trivia: Ponds were called "cow swamps" since cows were often found mired, or drown, in them.

TIPTONSPORT

Since Cass and White Counties were once a part of Carroll County, my next step was a trip to the Carroll County courthouse in Delphi, Indiana. Seeking the earliest records available, I was handed a book titled, "Deed Index Grantors #1 - Carroll County 1828. On August 11,1828 the first land in Carroll County, and also in the new town of Tiptonsport, Rock Creek Township # 26, was sold to the public. In that book I discovered evidence of Samuel Chappel, the veteran of the War of 1812, my great, great grandfather. In an item dated Aug. 29,1833, his name appeared in a government land grant book as the seller of lots. It did not show when, or how he acquired the property. If he had received Bounty Land Grants, for serving his country during the War of 1812, it could have led to his war records and to his place of origin. Instead I discovered Tiptonsport, a town where he once lived, a town that no longer exists. It showed that Samuel sold three of eighteen lots he had acquired in that newly established town. The lots sold for $ 90.00 each. By 1836 they had appreciated in value to $100.00 each. Records also showed that he owned most of the lots. He also owned an island in the middle of the Wabash River; known as Grundy's Island.

My next stop was at the Carroll County Historical Museum, located in the courthouse basement. There I found the following: Land sold to finance the construction of the Michigan road prompted the establishment of the town of Tiptonsport. The town was located on the south side of the river, fifteen miles below Logansport and six miles above Delphi. It was laid out with eight streets, one hundred and twenty-seven lots, each measuring fifty-seven and one-half feet wide by one hundred and fifteen feet in length, and covered twenty-eight acres plus sixty rods. Bondee's Reserve, two sections of land, was located two miles below Tiptonsport. This belonged to an Indian lady named

Antoine Bondee, the daughter of a Potawatomi Indian chief, who had wed a French trapper.

Tiptonsport was proposed as the county seat of government for the newly established Carroll County, named for the last surviving signer of the Declaration of Independence. Due to political influence Delphi was chosen. Tiptonsport grew to include two taverns, a blacksmith shop, a wagon making shop, a doctor, minister, and a general store. No meat was sold but wild game was plentiful. Most dwellings were cabins, with half-a-dozen frame houses. Church services, school classes, and social affairs were held at the Merrick House, the local inn.

A stagecoach line ran parallel with the Wabash operated between Terre Haute and Fort Wayne. By 1826 mail delivery arrived. A mailman, following an Indian trail, earned $ 2.50 a week or $130.00 per year. He rode through high water, wind, and rain from Crawfordsville to Lafayette, and to "the mouth of the Eel" or Logansport. When service was extended to Fort Wayne, the mailman's salary was increased to $2.70 every two weeks. By 1827 thirty mail routes existed in Indiana. There are conflicts in dates as to when mail routes were established, however The Postal & Allied History of Carroll Co, by Dora Thomas Mayhill, lists Lafayette as established in 1827 and Tiptonsport in 1832.) Tiptonsport was listed as a post town seventy-one miles from Indianapolis, and six hundred and forty-four miles from Washington, D.C.

An old item I found scribbled in my notes read: * The Hoosier Genealogist 1998:

"Letters being held at the Logansport post office on July 1, 1833. If unclaimed within three months, the letters would be returned to the General Post Office as dead letters." Included on that list was the name Chappel. It could have been for Samuel. It was listed under "W" not under "C."

A "brisk" commerce was conducted from a large warehouse located on Samuel's island, which was described as "being at the head of navigation; 28 miles above Lafayette; fifteen miles below Logansport; 5 miles from Delphi. Flatboats, keelboats and steamboats plied the river. According to old tales, trees, abundant in nearby dense forest, were harvested and cordwood was sold to steamboat captains to stoke their boilers. After stacking the wood aboard ship, woodsmen tied their pole boats to the rear of the vessel to be towed behind with an extra supply of fuel. As fuel became exhausted, aboard ship, wood was transferred from the pole boat to the steamer. When the flat bottom boat was empty it was cut loose and the lumbermen "poled" their way back to homeport. Farmers rafted produce down the Wabash to the Ohio, and Mississippi River to New Orleans. They transported grain to Chicago via the Michigan Road. Old-time tales relate that steamboat operations ceased because the river became filled with fish weirs and nets place there by settlers to catch fish for their tables.

A stagecoach arrived twice daily until the Wabash - Erie Canal was constructed. With its arrival the stage line operated only during the winter months when ice closed the canal. When the Wabash -Erie Canal arrived in Logansport foresighted businessmen in Tiptonsport, including Samuel Chappel, moved to Logansport and Tiptonsport declined. Another town, called Frankfort, sprang up but settlers deserted it and moved on to new horizons.

In 1873 Adam Vangundia, the original landowner, petitioned the State of Indiana for the land to revert back to him. By 1916 only one old house remained in what had been Tiptonsport. It, too, gradually fell to rack and ruin. To get to the site today, one must obtain permission to cross a farmer fields.

Other settlements faded into oblivion due to the coming of the canal, namely: Camp Rice; New Beauty; Last chance; Rattlesnake; Dog Town; Tiptonia and Paragon. Paragon was described as being located one and one-half miles above Pittsburg on the south side of the river, and was named for a steamboat that plied the Wabash in 1830. Canal operations began in 1840; the same year that Wm. Henry Harrison won the election. * Source: "The Changing World." Newspaper items by Will Ball in 1940.

Finding no genealogy facts, I still considered the search rewarding and added the following notes:

A fifty-cent poll tax was levied in 1830. The tax on a horse was fifty cents and a quarter for an ox. A silver watch was twenty-five cents and a gold one was a dollar. Indiana's first toll road was a plank road running from the northwest part of the state to Fort Wayne. By 1833 Logansport had horse-drawn streetcars. Recognizing a picture in an old book as the limestone cliff that lays at the bottom of our lane, I studied the article. The cliff has a 25-foot drop to the river below at a spot called Cedar Rapids, named for the cedar trees that once lined the shore. The following story originated when questions arose as to where the Wabash- Erie Canal should be located.

Logansport and Peru had to prove to the state that Delphi was not the head of steamboat navigation. As legend goes, an enterprising businessman from Peru offered a bonus of fifteen barrels of whiskey to the owner of the first steamboat to arrive in Peru. Two captains, operating vessels out of Lafayette, were tempted by the potent potables and agreed to make the trip.

The Republican made the first attempt to navigate the upper Wabash. After passing Delphi it got stuck on a sandbar near Tiptonsport. Passengers and crew, except for the ladies, attached ropes and pulled the boat free. The next morning they arrived at Cedar Rapids, near Georgetown, seven miles below Logansport. High rapids and fall of the river created obstacles that prevented the boat from descending further. After four days the passengers abandoned ship. The captain and crew toiled on. Finally, a dozen yoke of oxen was brought to haul the Republican back to Logansport. It arrived there on July 4, 1834. A man named Towe claimed the honor for being the first steamboat captain to make a trip to Logansport. Years later, the hulk of the ship was discovered at the bottom of the river, at the confluence of the Wabash and Eel Rivers.

In 1835 the steamboat "Science" attempted the trip. It left Logansport with full steam, but could not make it through Cedar Rapids. The captain cast rosin, tar, and sides of bacon into the fire to create steam. He also tossed overboard two hundred barrels containing salt and flour. The unmanageable boat dodged stone formations, hitting some, but avoided being reefed on an up-coming island. It finally reached Miamisburg, Peru, and passed the mouth of the Mississinewa River and arrived at Chief Godfrey's Indian village. The chief passed out gifts and hoped that the trip would be the beginning of tourist travel to his village. The boat returned to Lafayette where the captain laid claim to having made the first successful steamboat excursion on the Wabash River. * Source: Ben F. Stuart's History of the Wabash Valley.

CENSUS REPORT

Next. I began a methodical search of all census reports I could find. The first census was conducted in 1790. It listed four million Americans with nine out of ten living on farms. A Samuel Chappel was registered in almost every state of the Union, as it existed at that time; one in both North and South Carolina; New York; New Hampshire; Vermont; Maryland, and Connecticut. I found the name Chappel spelled with both single and double Ls. I also found it as Schappel. From one census to another, in the same family, an L would often be dropped or one added. Often the L appeared before the E, which made the search confusing except that the index in most reference books noted that all are one and the same, or that either was correct.

Ancestors from Ireland were called Chapman. From Switzerland it was Chappuis. The French version is Chapatal de La. Interestingly, according to a cousin, a French ancestor, supposedly, accompanied Sieur de La Salle on his exploration of Lake Michigan and the Mississippi River. During their explorations, in describing their voyage, they noted the phrase "the turn of the south bend of the St. Joseph River." This later lent itself to the name of the city of South Bend, Indiana.

If an ancestor did accompany La Salle on that journey, which I have not documented, I may have walked where an ancestor trod centuries ago. We lived in northern Indiana at the time. After reading about an ancient oak tree located near South Bend, and always ready for an adventure, we went for a drive to locate it. Accompanying us was a young grandson, whose idol was Knute Rockne. (After reading a boyish version of Rockne's life four times.) He wanted to see the golden dome of the University of Notre Dame. We found the tree in a cemetery still alive. Steel props supported the sagging limbs. It was under that CHARTER OAK that La Salle met with a band of Illinois

Indians and negotiated a treaty that gave him free passage to explore the Mississippi River. La Salle was there in 1679. Calculating the present age of that grandson, we must have been there about 1972-73.

The same cousin wrote, "Bennet Chappell was in that unfortunate little band who came to Virginia, in 1585, to establish the Roanoke colony. He was included in the group that was left behind when the ship returned to England. When the ship came back to America, no trace of survivors could be found." - Again this may be family myth. It is undocumented.

I discovered that a Chappel fought in the Battle of Bunker Hill; served in the Continental Line; the Cavalry, Infantry, and as Ensign in the Navy. They served as Dragoons, Georgia Rangers, and as the "Commander of the Battleship Rattlesnake, licensed to go beyond the seas." * Listed in "Revolutionary War Bounty Land Grants Awarded by the Government." By Lloyd DeWitt Bockstruck.

A Samuel Chappel, private from North Carolina, received a 640-acre grant described as being "Within the limits of land allotted to officers and soldiers of the Continental Line." It was dated January 1786. It couldn't be the Sam for whom I'm searching. He wasn't born until 1792. Two Samuels, a father and son, both served in the Revolutionary War, and received grants. Benjamin Chappel, of New York, received a grant in Indiana in 1811, and he fought in the Battle of Tippecanoe. To show how confounding the search can be, another Benjamin, from N. Carolina, also received a one hundred acre grant in 1811.

I know that Samuel had children born in New York State, so discovering a Jonah, Nathaniel, and Joshua, all from N.Y.; I wondered if they could be brothers, or perhaps cousins. Because I had always heard that my ancestors came from North Carolina, I wondered if the Chappels in the following tale could be ancestors, or relatives. If not, it's still an interesting bit of Indiana history:

White Oak Springs Stockade was located on high ground beside the Trace, a path trampled by buffalo and early settlers. It was located in White River Township, Knox County, a mile from present Pike County and a day's journey from Vincennes. The fort was established, and owned, by a veteran of the Revolutionary War. It served as a hostel for travelers, mostly veterans and their families on their way to the Ohio Country to claim Bounty Lands. It served as outpost and powder base for the Territorial Militia from 1800 to 1817. When the militia was established every able-bodied man was required to serve when Indians went on the warpath. Often, when this happened the towns were stripped of men. A private's pay for serving in the militia from August 11 to September 12, 1812 was $ 8.88 cents. A corporal's was $9. 17, and a sergeant received $10,66. Fines for desertion could not exceed $50.00 and plus an obligation to march in the next tour.

At first ten families, bound by intermarriage, arrived at White Oak. The migrations continued for ten years. Among the early arrivals were Chappels from Perquiman County, N.C. In 1810 Joab Chappell, his wife, Elizabeth, and their two-year old infant, Perinah, arrived. Letter they wrote to family members back in N. C. induced them to join them. Jacob, his wife and small daughter arrived later. Jacob soon left the fort and built a cabin, six miles east of the stockade, along the trace in Monroe Township, Pike Co. After the massacre at Pigeon Roost, a settlement in Scott County, in which Indians killed twenty people, mostly women and children, Jacob, fearing an Indian attack, moved his family back to the stockade. The British encouraged Indian raids by paying a bounty for each scalp they turned in. In 1811, both Joab and Jacob volunteered and joined the militia. Both fought in the Battle of Tippecanoe, November 7, 1811. After the Indians were subdued, Jacob and his family returned to their cabin. The family now included a son, Stephen, born while his father was off fighting.

More Chappels arrived from Pasquotank, Co., N.C. Josiah, Elizabeth, and Stephen; Mary, or Polly, (nickname for Mary) Rogerson, John and Anna Chappel, schoolteachers, joined the group in 1811. Elliot Chappel came to claim a land grant, issued in 1810, and was accompanied by his wife and son. Chappels arrived by the droves. The names Elizabeth and Stephen were repeated often. Thomas Chappell (note spelling) also fought with six hundred volunteers, two hundred and fifty Federal troops, and sixty Kentuckians under Harrison. Settlers had to contend with Indian attacks. They were plagued with floods that washed away their homes and livestock, and during June and September of 1812 earthquakes occurred. Many settlers of White Oak Springs were descendants of Quakers from the Isle of Wright.

An old inventory sales slip showed that a cow sold for $12.62 and one-half cent, and a broom cost equally as much. The price of a mare was $ 24. 82 —and a half-cent, a pair of saddlebag cost the same. The price of a gun was $24.37 plus a half-cent. A waistcoat was $11.76; pantaloons $4.01; a shirt cost $1.33. To have a plow shaped was twelve and a half cent, and to irone (iron) a well bucket cost $1.25.

I found following information in the Indiana Historical collections, Vol. X11, Governor' Messages & Letters "by Logan Esary (page 467) Title Page "Madison Road No. 15" — Signed by Joshua Wilkinson, Pres./ Commissioner, and recorded on Dec. 1, 1822, amount paid on Dec. 17, Draft #36 in favor of Samuel Chappel, contractor $657.54 -and a half cent.

This has to be THE Samuel Chappel from Tiptonsport, my g.g. Grandfather. I discovered it in an Indiana Source Book, p 275, Madison Road #15 - Madison to Indianapolis via Vernon & Columbus.

SAMUEL CHAPPEL'S PROBATED WILL

The first thing I noticed was that the name was spelled with two Ls. The ink was faded making the old hand written document difficult to read. Probate Recorded, Book B, page 678, May 13, 1839, Final papers Nov.1843. Although it lists his birth as 10/2/1792, and death 1/9/1839 in Cass Co., no birthplace was noted. It summons his wife, Polly Chappell, and his children. It was odd to note the different states the children were born in. Martha was born in New York in1817; Stephen was born in Virginia in 1821; Mary b. N.Y., 1825; Orran b. N.Y. 1829; Minerva b. 1827 N.Y. and Amanda b. New Jersey 1831. Five were married in Cass County. The family relocated from New York to Virginia between 1817 and 1821; returned to N.Y. by 1825, moved to New Jersey by 1831, yet Samuel was made Captain in Indiana in 1820. He must have criss-crossed the country many times.

The will itemized fourteen lots in Tiptonsport and an Island lying in the middle of the Wabash River. They were to be sold, with proceeds going to his children. The following lists of personal properties, including their appraisal price, were to be retained by Polly, his wife: A grass scythe & 2 sneads -? $2.00; Blols -? Containing 500 -looks like pearls $37.00; a keg of Saree, 20 oz. $ 1.60 - could it be syrup? 3 bushel of potatoes $15.00; 3 bed coverings & 3 sheets $24.00; 1 bed and bedding $6.00; 1 looking glass .23 cents; 1 sheet and 1 teakettle $1.00; 1 cast Da Da 50 cents; 1 large iron Dutch oven and lid $1.25; 1 stew kettle 75 cents; 1 large skillet .50 cents, and 1 large pot $1.25 — Making a grand total of $93.17 and a half-cent. - Not knowing her maiden name, I have found no trace of Polly or what happened to her after Samuel died.

Noting that the administrator was Phillip Pollard, I returned to the Logansport Historical Museum and again scanned "The

Changing World" by Will Ball. The first account showed Pollard in Connersville, Fayette County, in 1831. He was licensed to sell merchandise, transported by steamboat to Tiptonsport, where he later moved and operated the P.P & Co. in a large warehouse on Samuel's island. I found an itemized inventory list, dated Dec. 1832, which included linen collars, five cents; F.S. gloves six cents, (could be fox skin) 11 teakettles, 14 boxes of window glass, 15 kegs of nails, 16 pieces of stove pipes and six stoves, weighing 400 lbs. 1 box of hats, 4 kegs with jugs, scythes, horse collars, Queen's Ware dishes, tin ware, ploughs, 1 tea caddy, 1 Bible, 1 bologna sausage, coffee, tea, soap, 687 lbs. of salt -cost $12.02 cents. In 1839 Pollard moved to Logansport and built a home at 629 E. Market Street.

Tiptonsport had fallen into decline, and by 1830 many settlers moved to Burnettesville, including my great grandfather, Stephen Chappel. For several years he operated a wagon-making shop near the Common's in Logansport. The Commons was a meadow where all settlers grazed their cattle.

Burnettsville was named for Abraham Burnett, the first white settler who migrated from New Jersey in 1831 to claim a land grant. He built a cabin near a creek, which now bears his name, Burnett's creek. His cabin was located near an Indian village, agrarian people who farmed vast acreage. Indian trails led to Lake Cicott, named for a French trader. Cicott established a trading post in the area and was known to have lived on the north shore of the Wabash River, east of present day Georgetown, where George Chamberlain built a tavern on the river. Burnett married Kaukeawa, the Indian chief's sister and fought with the Indians, against Harrison, at the Battle of Tippecanoe. After the battle the Indians moved to the area known as Buffalo. As early as 1832, Burnett's creek supplied power for a sawmill. This, and the rich farmland, attracted settlers. New settlements called Sharon and Farmington sprang up. In 1854 they were incorporated into the town of Burnettesville.

In 1852 Isaac Mahurin founded the Farmington Academy, there. It was later known as the Indiana Normal School, the first normal school in Indiana and fifth in the nation. In 1886 it moved to Indianapolis and became the nucleus for what became Butler University. The old white frame academy building was converted to a dwelling. An old picture shows an ancestor standing along side the building. A caption under the picture says "Aunt Mary Brown." She later moved to Upland where I visited her often as I was growing up.

The 1850 census of Cass County listed Stephen Chappel, his wife Elizabeth, and three sons, Austin, James, and Stephen. My grandfather William had not yet been born. The 1880 census lists Stephen, age 52, wagon maker; wife Elizabeth; and sons Austin age 32; William age 24, wagon maker; Joseph age 24, day laborer. Did William have a twin? It also listed a daughter, Fanny, age 13. I later discovered old school records for her and her brother, Stephen. They were students at New Seminary, Burnettsville, and both had perfect attendance records and not tardy for a four week period. Stephen also lived in Upland as I was growing up.

In the History of Cass Co. by Helms, page 858 I found an entrée by the Miami Baptist Church, in the area of Union Mills, Miami Twp. July 25, 1842: "It is agreed that members shall meet with the church branch in Logansport. A committee has been appointed to make plans for a house of worship." Stephen was listed as a committeeman. The new building was erected in 1848. Prior to joining the Logansport group, the church services were held in the woods, only during the summer months.

Another old superstitions: "A halo around the moon means rain within 8 hours. - Cut your logs for a new house in the full of the February moon so bed bugs will never molest the dwelling."

CHAPELLS WHO CROSSED THE SEA

My next search led me to a copy of "The Complete Book of Emigrants -1661 to 1699. On page 486, # 12, I discovered George Chappel, son of Samuel Chappel of Allingsey, Somerset, England, husbandman deceased. George was apprenticed to Richard Browning for four years, and sailed to Jamaica aboard the Abraham & Mary. He was also noted in "List of Emigrants to America 1600 - 1700." On March 16, 1634, he sailed to New England on the Chrystia, and was listed as a servant to Rev. John Cotton. John Cotton was born in Darby, England 12/4/1585, and graduated from Emmanuel College, Cambridge. He was Vicar of the Parrish of Boston, England from 1616 to 1633, but he did not conform. He founded parishioners to sail to New England and "was charged to take advise of them at Plymouth." George Chappel, servant To Rev. Cotton, was admitted to the church, as was his wife Marie. They are listed as Pioneers of the Commonwealth of Massachusetts.

Chappels came to America as indentured servants, or convent servants, and as noted,

"With few exceptions, they were persons of gentle blood entitled to coats of arms and crests. Often it was a younger son who could not inherit land, wealth or position. Although apprenticed or indentured, they were educated beyond the par in their day." It would take pages to list all the Chappels who sailed from England. They came as apprentice clothiers, weavers, tanners, blacksmiths, millwrights, carpenters, laborers, farmers, herdsmen, tradesmen, and innkeepers. They came with religious groups seeking freedom of religion, and some came merely for adventure. In exchange for passage fare they bonded themselves for three to four years.

Whether as bonded servant or apprentice it was a way to populate the country. They accompanied settlers and helped improve the land, and received land grants for their labor. The head of a family was allotted fifteen acres for himself, ten acres for his wife, and five for each child. A single man received fifteen acres, a house, corn, cattle, and farming tools. He was assisted and supported until his crops were raised. English nobility became wealthy landowners for recruiting indentured servants as settlers. They received two hundred acres for each head of a household, plus additional acreage for each family member. If an indentured servant died, or didn't fulfill his term, his wife was forced to serve out his time.

Appearing in "List of Convicted Rebels" on page 333, John Chappel, of Petherton, sailed on the ship Happy Return, of Pool, England, under Capt. Roger Wadham, 12/1685. He was sent to Barbados, or other of Her Majesty Plantation, for his part in the Monmouth Rebellion. Prisoners could be sold or disposed of upon arrival there to several persons mentioned in a list. On page 338 it was noted that on March 12, 1685, Rebel was transported, aboard the Jamaica Merchant, to America.

THE MONMOUTH REBELLION

James Scott, the illegitimate son of Charles 11 of England, was born in April of 1649. He married Ann Scott, Countess of Buccleuch, and in so doing became Duke of Buccleuch. It was claimed that Charles 11 was married to Scott's mother, but Charles denied this. However, Scott was made Duke of Monmouth in 1663. He was became Captain- General of the armed forces in 1678. In 1684 a failed attempt to kill Charles 11 forced the Duke of Monmouth to flee to Europe. When Charles died, 1685, his brother the Duke of York was proclaimed King James 11 of England. When a rebellion was fermented, due to James being Catholic, Monmouth returned home and recruited locals to fight against the King. John Churchill led the King's forces. He later became the Duke of Marlborough. The two forces met at Sedgemoor in Somerset in what was known as the last battle of English history to be fought with pitchforks. John, the rebel, was also from Somerset. It seems to be the family place of origin. As the battle turned against him. Monmouth disguised himself as a shepherd hoping to escape back to Europe. He was discovered hiding under a hedge, and was recognized. A badge of The Order of the Garter found in his pocket identified him. He was imprisoned and seven days later was executed.

In many villages, neighbors fought against neighbors. In the village of Corscombe, thirteen rebels were hung, their bodies dismembered, boiled in pitch, and publicly exhibited. One George Penne was given one hundred prisoners as part payment for helping put down the rebellion. He sold most of them to planters in the West Indies and in America. In a sense they became white slaves. After Monmouth's execution, James 11 punished the rebels who had followed him. Two hundred were condemned to death and eight hundred were transported to the

New World. Those of prominent families, and landowners, were sent to the West Indies as free emigrants to establish businesses. They made great fortunes. Others, who sailed on the boat Happy Return, spent their lives in poverty and degradation. After the failed rebellion, Catholic King James reigned for only three years. In 1688 he was forced to flee the country and was replaced by William and Mary.

Knowing that John sailed to America, I searched for him in the 1790 census, the first one in the U.S. It turned up several John Chappels, but due to the entrée dates and lapse of years, none could have been John the rebel.

Another thing that makes researching difficult is the old custom of naming. The first son was named for the father's father, the second son for the mother's father, and the third son was named for its father. So there are many Samuel Chappels, and Stephens, Williams, Thomas, Ambrose, Johns and etc.

THE GEORGIA RANGERS

Chapel men fought in the Revolutionary War, the War of 1812, Mexican War, and Civil War, both World War 1 and II. Jay Chappel, Hancel's brother, enlisted in the Navy on May 10, 1918 at Indianapolis. Records list him as a machinist. He was discharged March 3, 1919. He was twenty-six years and six months of age when he enlisted in the army for a three-year stint. His army records note he was a Marksman, National Mounted Horseman, and a Blacksmith. When he was discharged, January 13, 1921. He was issued $57.09 travel pay from Edgewood Arsenal, Md. to Logansport, In. Having noted in a previous chapter that a Christopher Chappel was a Private in the First Troops of Georgia Rangers, I decided to research the Georgia Rangers. "The Colonial Soldiers of South Carolina" - 1732 - 1774 noted that in The Treaty of Augusta, 1763, Georgia opened two million acres of "Ceded Land" for settlement; back country land, lying above the Little River, which was inhabited by Creek Indians. Colonist, mostly English gentlemen, received vast domains for recruiting setters to locate in the region. A settler could claim one hundred acres for himself and an additional fifty acres for each family member. The cost was five pounds sterling per hundred acres, paid when moving upon the claim. After the land was surveyed, he paid another five shillings per acre. Many settlers from Scotland and the Orkney Islands relocated to this area.

Royal Agents of the King wanted to retain, and protect, the lucrative fur trading business conducted in the region. They encouraged traders and Indians to ferment trouble to stop these settlements. Settlers were reluctant to take up arms against England preferring to live in peace among the trappers and Indians. Georgia became a powder keg ready to explode. The Rangers were organized to drive out dissenters, many of whom were squatters, and to keep the peace. Often dressed as Indians, they scouted the wilderness, traveling as far as to the Scioto River, near present day Columbus, Ohio. In August 1775 an assault on a Kings representative started the Revolutionary War in Georgia. Rangers marched in defense of the frontiers. They fought in the Battle of Detroit, the invasion of Canada, and at the Niagara Straits during that war.

In John Tipton's records I discovered that Indiana also had Ranger Troops. It was organized by William Henry Harrison in 1807 to patrol Indiana after several Indian massacres had occurred. Each Ranger provided his own mount and arms, and received a dollar a day as pay. During the war of 1812, four units were organized, with John Tipton commanding two troops.

I have scanned the pages of many books, often forgetting to note the source, but in an account of one of those Indian attacks, I recognized the name Buskirk, the maiden name of my great grandmother, Elizabeth Ward, the mother who nursed her son, Granville, during the Civil War. Thinking it might be an ancestor I noted, "Buskirk, an early pioneer in Jackson County, Indiana, and a neighbor were harvesting pumpkins when Indians attacked and murdered both men."

During that days search at the library, I discovered Indiana land grants, for services rendered during the Revolutionary War, had been issued to three soldiers named William Chappel, five-named Samuel, plus one Samuel who served on the USS Rattlesnake. This makes it difficult to pinpoint my Samuel's records. Some were granted as few as fifty acres of land; others 640 acres, or a whole section, for services extending from two-month duty, to as many as three years; from 1732 to 1792.

PIONEER SETTLERS OF MASSACHUSETTS

Since my earliest record of a Samuel Chappel was through the discovery of George, son of Samuel listed as he sailed to America; I directed my research to George. He was twenty years old when he sailed from London to America in 1634. He bore a certificate from the Justice of Peace and Ministers of the Parish of St. Egyd, Cripplegate, attesting that he had taken the oath of allegiance. With Rev. John Cotton, they were "Founders of St. John's Protestant Church, and were instructed to take their advise from those in Plymouth." They were pioneers of Massachusetts.

After the Civil War in England, in which Cromwell defeated the Royalist and beheaded the King, from three to four hundred prisoners, mostly Scotsmen, were shipped to America, as apprentices, actually in servitude. They were sold to planters, mill owner, etc, throughout the colonies and in the West Indies. The second consignment of these persons was distributed among towns in Massachusetts as cheap labor. In 1655 they petitioned the state for freedom, which was denied. Since Rev. John Cotton seemed to sanction the practice, it deadened the conscience of those securing such peonage.

In an endeavor to explain his position, Cotton wrote that he, "only desired to make their yoke easier." Many arrived sick with scurvy and other ailments, hardly able to work. Cotton insisted they should not be sold into perpetual servitude, but rather for a term of six to eight years. He persuaded those who bought them "to build them houses and layeth some acres of ground thereto for them for their own. They should only be required to work three days each week for those to whom they were indentured, and to have four days to work for themselves; to till their land; to earn money to repay for release from their indenture."

251

Cotton believed the Church and State should be partners. He opposed democracy, or the people's rule. He believed the people should choose their leaders and, "they should rule accordingly." He opposed the Calvinist and the political views of Roger Williams, founder of the Rhode Island colony. At first he defended Ann Hutchinson, whose son had also sailed to America with him. He later turned against her.

Another type of bondage was instituted to supply manpower and to secure settlers for the colonies. Between 1614 and 1775, thousand of English men, women, and children were deported to America for crimes ranging from theft of a handkerchief, bigamy, and highway robbery. One Ambrose Chappel, from Somerset, age fourteen arrived in 1731 with such a group. - Somerset again! It has to be an ancestor. Ambrose only shows one cannot pick and choose their ancestors. As is said, be they rogue, rascal or saint they cannot be extricated from family genealogy. The Chappel clan seems to have had its share of all, which makes the searching more interesting.

At a recent genealogy seminar a lady cautioned against tracing ancestors who have served time in prison, saying, "I did and the FBI came knocking at my door." But besides Ambrose, who might be considered a black sheep of the family, there was a long ago William Chappel DD, born in Nottingham, England in 1582 who was Bishop of Cork. Educated at Mansfield and Christ Church, he was Dean of Cashel, Ireland in 1633, and later at Trinity College, Dublin, and "he suffered many hardships of rebellion." When he returned to England he was sent to prison, but granted his freedom, "he wrote many articles of faith and scripture." Another son of Sam, in 1809 pioneered English musical research. He established a piano manufacturing company in London's Bond Street; founded the Philharmonic Society, and the building of St. James Concert Hall in 1858. He wrote, and published, a collection of national and traditional English songs. So Chappels, and Chappells, were surely saints and sinners! During this search, although not looking for it, as often happens, I rediscovered John, the Monmouth rebel. As I scanned the pages of "Cavaliers and Pioneers - Abstracts of Virginia Land Patents and Grants 1623-1666" by Nell Marion Nugent, I discovered that John was reprieved and sailed from Barbados to America in 1694. (Monmouth rebellion 1684) He, and twenty-three other persons, received land, "out of 1150 acres ceded by Robert Newman, described as lying on the Potomeck River, (Potomac) in Northumberland County."—

Then I found it! Samuel Chappel, Seaman, War of 1812, captured by English. Confined Dartmoor Prison, England. Released 1806. But he was born in 1783. Disappointment, the Sam for whom I'm searching was born 1792. - Could there be an error?

BOUNTY LANDS

Stymied in my pursuit of Samuel, I turned my focus to locating early Kirk family members, since my great grandmother had married a Kirk. While not truly ancestors, childhood tales have interwoven them into the fabric of our family history. A visit to the Rensselaer library turned up the following information: "Indiana Land Entries, Vincennes District"- 1807-1877, by Waters, I discovered that one hundred and twenty eight grants of "Donated Lands "were issued in Gibson County on August 1, 1790. One Hundred acres were allotted to each man enrolled, soldiers who had served in the militia at Vincennes with George Rogers Clark. Edmond and James Crow Kirk's names appeared as having received such grants.

Further: "A Census of Indiana Territory "written by Richard B. Kirk 1807 listed Henry Kirk, pioneer, came to the area prior to Jasper becoming a county in 1838. It noted: "The first cabin built in the area, by a white man was erected in Gillian County in 1836." Jasper Counties third courthouse burned down March 16, 1843 so many records were lost. But I searched on: When early pioneers arrived, Spain still controlled land in the southwest. Dreading the flow of settlers across the Mississippi River, they armed the Indians and encouraged them to raid villages, massacre the white, and deter their advancement. The Kirk brothers migrated from North Carolina by following the Warrior Road through the Cumberland Gap. The Wilderness Road, blazed into the territory wasn't opened until 1796. Kentucky became the fifteenth state in 1792, and many who first settled in Kentucky eventually moved on to Indiana to established homes.

These hardy people came for many reasons but mainly because, in 1790, the top ten per-cent of the population controlled half the land, also the cash, in America. Land hungry masses were forced to move on. The Louisiana Purchase had not yet been consummated; this was about one-fourth of the land in the U.S. So the Bounty Land Act was passed in 1812 in lieu of payment to soldiers. Fire Lands were given to people whose property, and homes, were destroyed by fire during the War of 1812, when the British burned the White House. Although historical tales relate how Dolly Madison wrapped the china, and silverware in red velvet drapes, removed the picture of George Washington from the wall, and the original copy of the Declaration of Independence, and escaped with them, many were usable to rescuer treasures and save their homes. They were repaid in Fire Lands.

After the War of 1812 people demanded better roads. Congress appropriated money for new ones, improved existing ones, and to build a canal "connecting the waters of the Wabash to those of Lake Erie." John Tipton, U. S. Senator from Indiana 1831-1839, acted as Chairman of Roads and Canals. As Indiana's State Representative 1819 - 1923, Tipton was instrumental in the state capital being moved from Corydon to Indianapolis. This was delayed due to the Blackhawk Wars. Tipton helped determine boundary lines between Illinois and Indiana. (1821)

In connection with the Wabash-Erie Canal, my our old abstract of title shows, "the 19th and 21st. Congress, March 2, 1827, granted 29,528.78 acres of land for the Wabash- Erie Canal, approved May29, 1830 by President Andrew Jackson. Land not used for the canal will be sold by the State with fee simple title." Later the 28th congress extended a five-mile wide strip on each side of the canal. Another entrée in the abstract notes: "On April 3, 1901 a two year option for the right or privilege, in perpetuity, across the Wabash River at Cicott's Reserve, to construct a dam, not to exceed eleven feet above the surface of the water." Had this option been exercised, the landscape from my windows would be vastly different today. From my front window, almost at the point of the proposed dam, the river flows by un-hampered. From my kitchen window I can see a row of trees that mark channel of the old canal and down the road, at the Tow Path Labor Training Camp, remnants of that old canal, with water in it, are still visible.

Before the canal came, there was a small settlement called Barnesville. James Barnes established it in 1830, as a fur trading post. To eradicate wolves, Barnes paid a dollar for each scalp turned in. He hauled furs and hides, wild game meats, nuts and ginseng to Cincinnati via the Michigan and National Roads. He also conducted a thriving local trade. Barnesville faded away, and after the canal opened, Rockport sprang up and business boomed. Harness shops, blacksmith shops; cabinet and cooper shops, and warehouses sprang up. Taverns, and liquor stores thrived, with liquor selling for 18 and a half cent a quart. By 1838 Rockport had became the hub of commerce. Today it is a quite crossroad community with a small cluster of houses. Before these shops existed pioneers imported nails, pots and pans, horseshoes, scythes, plows, and weapons. Most were shipped from England requiring as long as and fourteen weeks in transit.

Another early settlement in the area was Amsterdam. It was also the site of the first mill, built by George Cicott in 1829. In 1835 the name Amsterdam was changed to Georgetown, when a Dr. Gordon settled in the area. Gordon operated a department store. Business was so brisk he employed a dozen clerks. He toiled improving the town for thirty-three years, but when the canal went defunct, his operation failed and he died penniless. The first rail link to a major river port was completed from Madison to Indianapolis. With the coming of the railroads, the canal towns were doomed.

Most of these facts have little to do with genealogy, but being a latecomer to the region, as I browsed for family facts, I discovered history that gives me new insight to my surroundings. I even enjoyed the trivia. - How else would I know that during the early days a quarter was called a shinplaster? Or that within ten years after firearms were introduced to the Indians, most abandoned their tomahawks and bows and arrows for guns. And that, not until 1923 did Congress pass The Indian Citizenship Act.

I found another avenue to explore; The Militia Census passed in 1806. The government, anticipating another conflict with England, required that all males, ages sixteen to eighteen and from eighteen to forty-six to register. - Another blank. Samuel would have been fourteen years old, too young for the census.

JULIA V. DAWSON

JOHN CHAPPEL, CAPTAIN OF THE SPEEDWELL

As I explored the pages of "A List of Emigrants to America "1600 - 1700 I discovered a John Chappel, Captain of the Speedwell, licensed to go beyond the seas. On July 24, 1635, at age thirty-eight, he sailed to Virginia. Further research showed the Speedwell was the sister ship of the Mayflower.

In 1608 British Pilgrims fled from England to Holland to escape persecution for their religious beliefs. They settled in Leiden, where Dutch Calvinist granted them haven. The group of dissenters included William Brewster. After printing articles critical to British authorities, he was force to flee and his press was shut down. Spanish soldiers had been stationed in Leiden following problems between Holland and Spain. They were charged with guarding and protecting the Pilgrims. Among the group was a soldier named Miles Standish. He eventually adopted their beliefs and joined their group.

Through an agreement with England's Plymouth Company, the Pilgrims, (actually this mean any settler) were given a charter to settle on the eastern seaboard of America. A group of settlers from England were to sail for America on the Mayflower. Those from Leiden, called the Leiden Separatists, were to sail from Holland on its sister ship, the Speedwell, with John Chappel as captain. The Speedwell sailed to England and both ships left England on July 22, 1620. However, both vessels were forced to return to Southampton, England when the Speedwell developed leaks. Finally the thirty-five passengers from the Speedwell were taken aboard the Mayflower. Two months later they arrived in Plymouth. The Speedwell arrived a week later. Among its passengers was William Bradford, who became the governor of the Plymouth Colony. * Source: Encyclopedias and various references by Bradford.

Later, in studying a list of Quakers I mentally noted the name Austin Chappel. I remembered it because my grandfather had a brother named Austin.

After a trip to the National Archives, in Washington, D.C., a cousin passed on the following information: Samuel Chappel, N.Y. Militia, 27th Regiment under Shoemaker. He included no details. I know that Samuel was born in N.Y., as were several of his children. For the present I'll assume this is the Sam I seek. But I will continue the search. Now that I have acquired a computer, the World Wide Web offers many avenues to explore. - I've already learned the name Chappel, with 10,794 listings, is the most popular name in the U.S. While dates and events are not always listed in chronological order, they are listed in the order in which I discovered them. Although began as a family genealogy research, it was continued for the interesting, and historic tales uncovered.

ABOUT THE AUTHOR

When faced with the empty nest syndrome, after raising three children, Julia worked as a licensed real-state agent in northwest Indiana. When, at age fifty-nine, her husband announced he was taking early retirement in order to travel the continent in a recreational vehicle, Julia recorded their vast experiences. Those tales are currently appearing in her weekly "Time Traveler" column in the Logansport Pharos Tribune.

After attending Elderhostel sessions at the University of Iowa in "Writing Your Memoirs" she wrote "Hancel ", a story of her mother. Later a seminar on genealogy inspired her to ad the prequel, "Ancestors Of Yore."

When her husband, of sixty-four years, died in November of 2000, Julia, to keep occupied, bought a computer, reworked the tales and decided to try the new print on demand method of publishing her book.

Julia is an avid basketball fan and her hobbies include gardening; activities with her great grandchildren and writing and researching genealogy. Via the World Wide Web, she has recently made contact with distant family members connected through their great-great-grandfather Samuel Chappel. One cousin from California recently visited her in Indiana May of 2001.

Printed in the United States
5070

9 780759 658974